JERZYK

Diaries, Texts and Testimonies
of the Urman Family

JERZYK

I'm Not Even a Grown-up
THE DIARY AND DIARY FRAGMENTS OF JERZY FELIKS URMAN

May the Blood
THE DIARY OF (AND OTHER TEXTS BY) SOPHIE URMAN

The Aktion Is Over
THE TESTIMONY OF IZYDOR URMAN

Edited, Introduced and Annotated by Anthony Rudolf

Translator and Consultant Editor – Antonia Lloyd-Jones

Shearsman Books

Published in the United Kingdom in 2016 by
Shearsman Books
50 Westons Hill Drive
Emersons Green
BRISTOL
BS16 7DF

Shearsman Books Ltd Registered Office
30–31 St. James Place, Mangotsfield, Bristol BS16 9JB
(this address not for correspondence)

ISBN 978-1-84861-369-0

Parts of this book, including the earlier translation of
I'm Not Even a Grown-up: The Diary of Jerzy Feliks Urman,
were first published by King's College London/Menard Press in 1991.

CONTENTS

So we lived
And chose to live

These were our times.
                    —George Oppen

In memoriam:
the unknown and forgotten children
– of all religions and none –
murdered 'over there'
by 'the Nazi beast'.[1]

---

[1] Quotes from David Grossman's *See Under: Love* (1990).

Acknowledgements (2016)

I would like to thank my friend and expert on matters Polish, Antonia Lloyd-Jones, for agreeing to serve as Consultant Editor of this revised and greatly expanded book, for translating Sophie Urman's diary and Izydor Urman's testimony (and the biographical note on Emil Urman in that section), for revising the translation of Jerzy Feliks Urman's (Jerzyk's) diary, and for helping me with the preparation and revision of notes. Any departure from her proposed phraseology is my responsibility. Thanks are due to Jerzyk's sister, Irit Smith, for information, photographs and unstinting support, to W. D. Jackson for his comments on a draft of the new introduction as well as his translation of the German passages in Sophie's diary, to Dirk Wilutzky and Mathilde Bonnefoy concerning one German passage, and to Sergey Kravtsov, Sharman Kadish, Miriam Neiger, Mary Krom, Jennie Feldman, Frank Hellner, Howard Cooper, Mick Jaron, and Claude Vigée for discussing with me the Hebrew texts on the gravestone photograph and the Hebrew accompanying it in the Tłumacz memorial book. Thanks also to Andrzej Paczkowski, Nina Karsov, and Michael Pinto-Duschinsky for help with the note about the mysterious 'Syrenka' in Sophie's diary and the one about reprisals in Jerzyk's diary fragments, and to Michael, again, and Antony Polonsky, for thinking about the Polish wording and dates on Hermina Urman's tombstone. Thanks to Antony Gray and Aloma Halter for copying material, and to Mike Fliderbaum, Steven Jaron, Paula Rego, and Tomek Wiśniewski concerning photographs. I thank Dr Wojciech Płosa, head of Archives at the Auschwitz–Birkenau State Museum in Oświęcim, and the International Tracing Service in Bad Arolsen. Many thanks also to Joshua Bernhardt and Emmanuelle Moscovitz and other colleagues at Yad Vashem in Jerusalem for help with research. Special thanks to Beate Schützmann-Krebs for tracking down photographs. Finally, gratitude to Tony Frazer for knowing this book had to be published, and to Ayesha Chari, copy-editor supreme; the manuscript of this book presented exceptional problems and I was fortunate to have her professional support.

First Edition Acknowledgements (1991)

As will be clear from my Introduction, I could not have edited this book without the support and encouragement of my cousin Dr Izydor Urman and his wife Sophie in Tel Aviv. Every parent's worst nightmare is to be predeceased by a child. Sophie and Izydor experienced this, and in the most unbearable way. I know they respect and understand the underlying reasons for my work and why I had to ask so many questions over the years. At last, with the publication of his diary, Jerzyk can echo the proud Latin words of the Warsaw Ghetto doctors who investigated the effects of starvation on their patients and on themselves, and whose manuscript was found after the war: '*Non omnis moriar*' ('I shall not wholly die'). As it happens, those words were written in Warsaw just as Jerzyk was leaving Stanisławów for Drohobycz. Izydor and Sophie – reflecting their respective ways of surviving into the future (and into the past) – shared different kinds of information with me. Sophie's memoir was written in English for a class she was taking; I have edited it where necessary. All conclusions about established (and sometimes un-established) facts have been drawn by myself. Even though this book only exists as a result of their commitment, they bear no responsibility whatsoever for the editorial and authorial presentation.

I am pleased to acknowledge the help of friends, relatives and colleagues. In Israel: Nommi Gerstel, Misha Greenberg, Leah Hahn, Gabriel Moked, Dov Noy and Ora Alkalay (head librarian of Yad Vashem). In the USA: Joachim Nachbar (who allowed me to use the ghetto map from his family book on Stanisławów), Zygfryd Rudolf, and Samuel Norich and colleagues at the Yivo Institute, New York. In Austria: Elisabeth Freundlich and Gitta Deutsch. In Hungary: Ernest Beck. In the Soviet Union: Rabbi Victor Kalesnik, Ludmilla Maltseeva, Alfred Schreier, Volodya Tsimberg. In the UK: Merlin James, for his careful and constructive comments. Also, Felix Raphael Scharf, Joanna Voit, John Roberts, Michael May, Mike Popham, Deborah Maccoby, Keith Bosley, Barbara Garvin, Rabbi Edward Jackson, Liz James, Marius Kociejowski, Tom Pickard, Donald Rayfield, Ken Smith, Judy Trotter, and Moris Farhi.

[Some of those named have died or may have died since the above was written.]

Editor's Note (2016)

This book contains several accounts of the same events experienced by one family – quite a rare if not unique multiple perspective in the literature of the Second World War. Inevitably, primary information and/or editorial comment is repeated. When in doubt, leave it in, has been my watchword. With material of such potency, I felt it was essential to attempt to come at the truth from as many angles as possible. Naturally, I sought help from written sources as well as from the individual authorities I have named in the acknowledgements.

I decided to present the different documents and statements in their original form together with detailed explanatory footnotes and brief introductions. This approach should enable readers to interpret for themselves the implications of the diaries and the other accounts of the death of one child.

This is why I did not attempt the role of storyteller nor use the patchwork of evidence to provide a chronological account or a linear narrative about the events in eastern Poland before and after and, especially, during the critical years from 1941 to 1944.

Mistakes or illogicalities or doubts or disagreements in respect of points in the notes and introductions should be conveyed to the editor, who will incorporate demonstrable improvements in any reprint or online versions in future. I would be particularly grateful if any reader could explain the word 'syrenka' found in Sophie's diary.

Owing to the vast number of notes relative to the length of texts, I decided to present the notes at the end of each section rather than on the page itself. Any readers this book finds will surely not mind keeping a finger in the relevant notes while reading the text.

The text of the new introduction is revised from a previously unpublished talk given during a conference on 'Holocaust Writing and Translation' at the Institute of Germanic and Romance Studies, School of Advanced Study (SAS), University of London, UK, 24 February 2011.

Note that all editorial interventions and translator's interpretations (new to this edition and/or when in doubt) are included throughout in italicised text within square brackets, differentiated from Emil Urman's additions and/ or clarifications in Jerzyk's diary and diary fragments as un-italicised text in square brackets or between '/ /' marks. As explained where relevant, there is some confusion about the dates/days of some entries in both Sophie's and Jerzyk's diaries. For the reader's ease, editorial liberty has been taken to complete (but not correct) incomplete date entries and maintain consistency in format.

Also for the reader's ease, editorial norms have been followed as far as possible with regard to standardisations, such as the use of italics for foreign words/phrases unfamiliar in the English language; large sections and familiar (foreign) proper nouns have been set in Roman type. Any other standardisations are solely for the reader's clarity, and have been made with great care to maintain – as does the translation – the integrity of the original manuscripts.

PART I

*Introductions and Notes to the First (1991)
and Second (2016) Edition
of the Diary and Diary Fragments
of Jerzy Feliks Urman*

New Introduction (2016)

1

Jerzy Feliks Urman (known as Jerzyk) was my second cousin once removed. He was born on 9 April 1932 in Stanisławów (now Ivano-Frankivsk) in East Galicia, Poland (now western Ukraine). During the German occupation of his homeland, he kept a diary (full entries and fragments) from 10 September until 12 November 1943, the day before he died. The boy was in hiding with four other people: his parents Sophie and Izydor Urman, his paternal uncle Emil Urman (some of the time), and his paternal grandmother Hermina Vogel Urman. The tragic events took place in Drohobycz (now Drohobych), a small town with a major oil refinery: another paternal uncle, Artur Urman, had a senior post in the refinery from before 1939. Drohobycz was the home town of that great Polish-language writer Bruno Schulz, who was murdered by a Nazi in November 1942. It is clear from all the literature that East Galicia, Jerzyk's homeland, hosted more enthusiastic collaboration by the local population (against Jews and also Poles) than anywhere else in Europe. It also hosted some of the cruellest *Aktionen* and sadistic killings. However, it is right to mention the head of the Ukrainian Greek Catholic church, Archbishop Sheptytsky of Lwów (now Lviv), who took the audacious step of addressing a letter to Heinrich Himmler protesting what Himmler would have called the exterminations.

Jerzyk's diary is written in Polish. It spans only two months because Jerzyk killed himself with cyanide at the age of eleven and a half, the only child suicide in the entire records of Yad Vashem. Notwithstanding the arguments of Lawrence Langer and other writers who see resistance purely in military terms, I regard the keeping of Jerzyk's diary and the manner of his death as acts of resistance, resistance of the noblest and most tragic kind. Although Jerzyk was precocious, clear-sighted, and sharp-witted, the diary is not a work of literature. Nor is it even the work of a future writer (with the possible exception of the two entries in the 'Pink Notebook'; see p. 101), unlike, for example, the diary of Anne Frank. It is, however, a document of considerable interest beyond the heart-rending fact of its existence. It is an intelligent child's truthful account of experiences and states such as threat and rumour, nervous energy and fear, pain and insight. He kept the diary, he said, because he wanted people afterwards to know what happened.

Sadly but truthfully, the diary was a gift to someone like myself who was already writing what would later become short books and essays about Primo Levi, Piotr Rawicz, and other Holocaust survivors. You could say I was obsessed with the territory. Most important of all, I was the only person in the world close enough to Jerzyk's parents – yes, they survived the war – to obtain moral and legal permission to translate and edit his diary. In theory his sister Irit, born soon after the war, could have done the research, but in practice she was emotionally too close to the situation. As editor, publisher, and co-translator of the first version of the diary, I, who on the strength of the photographic evidence even looked like Jerzyk when I was young, was able to ensure that his verbal remains survive out in the open, not resting quietly in a folder in Yad Vashem – the Holocaust memorial museum and library in Jerusalem – where I first saw his Uncle Emil's diary transcript and his father's and uncle's testimonies.[1] I like to think the gift was returned to the world with the publication in 1991 of *I'm Not Even a Grown-up: The Diary of Jerzy Feliks Urman*: 'I'm not a writer, I'm not even a grown-up'.[2]

The document in Yad Vashem was a photocopy of the transcript of the diary typed by Emil, after the war (perhaps in Poland, perhaps in Israel), and which Jerzyk's parents had placed in the museum for posterity, along with Izydor's own testimony, specially prepared to accompany the diary, and the document by Emil. Sophie was sure the original was also in Yad Vashem, but the library told me they had returned it to the family. Yet, it was nowhere to be found. However, it finally turned up in Sophie's apartment on Klonimos Street when she was about to move from Tel Aviv to be near her daughter in Florida, some years after the first edition was published. It was nearly thrown away but fortunately she spotted it and saved it from a zealous cleaning lady. I now own the original, a precious family heirloom, which will end up in Yad Vashem one day.

2

With the help of Antonia Lloyd-Jones (who revised parts of the original translation), I have prepared this new book which contains the revised version of Jerzyk's diary and other material from the 1991 edition, as well as the previously unpublished material by Izydor and Emil and, above all, the hitherto undiscovered diary of Sophie. In this attempt to come even closer to the truth, I now see problems of motive and action I had not worried about enough at the time, and hope I have found answers to certain questions I raised in my introduction to the first edition, answers that had to await the rediscovery of the original manuscript of Jerzyk's diary. For example, as indicated in the first edition, there are comments in parentheses in the transcript: we now know these were added by Emil to clarify his nephew's words. Other issues include the confused dating of certain entries. My editorial apparatus in the first edition took up more space than Jerzyk's short diary and his mother's account – an article she wrote for an English language class – combined, but how could it be otherwise, given an editor's responsibilities in this field?

As stated, I am publishing for the first time Izydor's testimony with two additional texts, one of them Sophie's diary and the other an interview Sophie gave in English two years after the book came out,[3] in which she shifts her ground and appears to blame her husband for Jerzyk's death by implying that he alone had allowed the boy to have the pill rather than explaining the extraordinary and desperate circumstances in which solo possession of cyanide by each individual had been agreed with Jerzyk, for reasons I shall explain in section '3' below. She shifted her ground because people had criticised her after reading the first edition of Jerzyk's diary. Her precise words can be read in the interview, as printed in this volume (p. 73). As for Sophie's diary, while clearing out her mother's flat in Florida after her death in 2003 (Sophie moved there in 1993 following the death of Izydor in Tel-Aviv in 1991), her daughter Irit found the diary Sophie herself had kept under the occupation, beginning a few weeks after Jerzyk died. No one, not even Irit, had been aware of the existence of this important document, now published for the first time in the translation by Antonia Lloyd-Jones.

Quite clearly, part of the intense drama associated with the diary and the short life of my cousin resides in the fact that his parents and one of his two uncles survived the occupation and the war, as did his grandmother; they all ended up in Israel except for his grandmother, who died in Poland in 1950. On several occasions in the 1970s and 1980s, I met Izydor and Sophie in north Tel Aviv. I have told the back story of our relationship in a small book that accompanied the first edition of the diary, *Wine from Two Glasses* (1991).[4] There are minor discrepancies between *I'm Not Even a Grown-up* and *Wine from Two Glasses*, because I deliberately excluded the post-war parental drama from the former. I never showed the second book to Izydor and Sophie in order to preserve *shalom bayit*, to use the Hebrew phrase for an old Jewish precept, the peace of the house, domestic harmony, something I disturbed on more than one visit.

My relationship with Jerzyk's parents was complicated, inevitably so. Izydor told me what he could bear to tell me, and gave me a copy of the Yad Vashem testimony and an Israeli Polish newspaper summary of it (clearly his shortened authorised version). He supported my project but understandably – if you have seen *Shoah* (1985) and other films containing survivor interviews – wanted no direct involvement and angrily forbade his wife from further discussion with me. I did my best to persuade him that, if I was to do my job properly, eyewitness accounts such as Jerzyk's were crucial to the historiography of the war against the Jews and I needed to know *everything* that could be known, but I knew it would mean returning Izydor and Sophie into the pit of memory and sorrow.

Izydor willed the end, but not the means. He wanted his son's diary to survive and was not opposed to the idea of a translation. After all, it was he who informed me about the transcript of the diary offered to Yad Vashem and which was accepted by the museum after the original had been inspected. He told me a few things before he clammed up. It was not easy to be married to Izydor. He was by nature and force of circumstance moody, finally and understandably retreating into depression and silence, whereas Sophie had a sunnier disposition. There came a point when Izydor put his foot down: no more discussions. I did not know how to proceed and feared the project might never be completed. But, a couple of days later, Sophie phoned me at my hotel and we arranged to meet secretly in Kassit, a coffee house (now vanished) on Dizengoff Street, which I already knew well as a rendezvous for poets and intellectuals.

In Kassit, she gave me an unpublished text she had written for the English language class already mentioned: I edited it, and it later served as a second introduction to the diary and is, of course, included in this edition. Henceforth she and I were involved in a conspiracy, a benign conspiracy, serving the interests of history and memory. She phoned me once or twice at the hotel, fearful that her husband suspected she and I had met. But she got away with it, answered my questions in person and in letters and on the phone to London. She understood, I believe, that as a writer – who had been born in 'the safety' of unoccupied London in September 1942, after the Blitz and before the V-1 and V-2 attacks (see the appendix to this book as well as remarks in her diary: p. 48) – and as a relative of Jerzyk, I was fascinated by his life and death and, most importantly, was committed to the truth. She drew the line at accompanying me on one of my two trips to Western Ukraine, where indeed, as recounted in my book *Wine from Two Glasses* and in the introduction to the first edition of the diary, I visited the room in which Jerzyk died.

3

I know that the terrible burden of the parents lay not only in the fact that Jerzyk killed himself but also in that they survived, so they believed, because their son died. As I said earlier, people criticised Sophie for permitting Jerzyk to have cyanide on him. So, why did he have it? Together and separately, his parents explained the background (and some of it is described in Izydor's testimony; see pp. 85-6). Some time between April and August 1942, when they were living in the Stanisławów ghetto – where only the cat enjoyed himself, thanks to ghetto rats and milk supplied by guards – the boy had witnessed an atrocity: a child's eye was gouged out with a red-hot wire because he had been caught smuggling. The boy had also seen members of the *Judenrat* (the Jewish Council) hanging from a pole. Jerzyk, then aged ten and already in some respects a man, refused to go into hiding without promise of his own portion of cyanide: he was afraid that if caught he would give away, under torture, information such as the hiding places of friends. Izydor as a doctor and gynaecologist had access to the product and one writer tells us that it was easily, if expensively, obtainable on the black market: it saved the Germans expenditure on bullets. That the boy, in my opinion rightly or at least understandably, had the cyanide on his person, and that it had been agreed with him they would all take the cyanide if captured, tells us all we need to know about the war against the Jews In October, the family finally fled to Drohobycz – where a hiding place had been arranged (see p. 31) – having through cunning and luck avoided death in the Stanisławów ghetto and Bełżec, the nearest death camp, which would later have only a handful of survivors.[5]

Jerzyk made the wrong call at a specific moment. This does not derogate from his heroism. During his thirteen months in hiding (eight months in the final room), the only member of the family who could go out was Sophie, as she was able to masquerade as a pious Catholic, attend church because she did not look Jewish, and even be employed. Jerzyk died on 13 November 1943 – a few months after the justified optimism that the victory at Stalingrad engendered in Izydor about the war's outcome – because he misinterpreted a knock on the door. According to his parents, Jerzyk must have assumed it was the Gestapo following a possible tip off about their hiding place and this was preying heavily on his mind (see *Sophie's Diary*: p. 47), but it turned out to be Kripos, local militia, ethnic German or Silesian Polish collaborators to whom they had been betrayed by two of the three or four people they thought they could trust, if only on financial grounds. The Kripos witnessed Jerzyk take the pill and were so shocked that they ran off, saying they would return later. This enabled the parents to bury their son in the garden during the night. The opportunistic collaborators returned a week later, but allowed the four survivors to live perhaps because they knew their war was going to be lost and they feared retribution.[6]

Although the family had agreed in principle that they would survive together or die together, when it came to the crunch, in Sophie's words, they 'did not have enough strength to die by poison'. Ever since, how could they not believe that they survived because Jerzyk died, even if other factors played a role? In any case, nothing could bring him back. Still, there was one way to live forwards: make a new life, exemplifying the theologian Emil Fackenheim's famous imperative, the six hundred and fourteenth commandment, namely no posthumous victories for Hitler.[7] In August 1944, Izydor and Sophie endured the pain of digging up their son and reburying him in the Jewish cemetery in Drohobycz.[8] Their daughter Irit was born on 29 October 1945. Soon after, they moved to Bytom in Poland, where Izydor worked as a gynaecologist. In 1947, they left for Paris before, finally, in 1949 settling in Israel, where Sophie's parents had gone before the war. Izydor's mother died in Bytom in 1950, at which point Emil left Poland for Israel. By now, many journals and diaries of Holocaust survivors and victims have been published, and Jerzyk's belongs on the same shelf as other youthful testimonies[9] as well as *The Diary of Adam's Father*.[10]

Now we come to the original translation of Jerzyk's diary. A friend of mine, the poet Tom Pickard, was married to a Polish lady, Joanna Voit: she worked with me on the transcript. (I have done a lot of translation, from languages I know well and, with help, from languages I do not know well or at all.) Anything not clear could be glossed in a factual note. The problems were the inconsistencies and complications already alluded to, but many of these, along with some mistakes, have at last been resolved with the help of Antonia Lloyd-Jones, now that she has been able to revise the translation directly from the original manuscript which no one had access to in 1990. I reflect sombrely that Jerzyk was only ten years older than me – at the time of publication he would be nearly eighty-four – and could have survived the war, with or without a longer diary, but with his life, and what conversations we would have had.

Let me describe one entry in Jerzyk's diary, the only one that coincides with a date in Anne Frank's diary, namely 10 September 1943, when they both report the news of the capitulation of Italy and with the same optimism. Anne had been listening to the Dutch Service of the BBC. Jerzyk had almost certainly been listening to the Polish Service. Jerzyk's diary entry tells us that the local newspaper did not give much prominence to 'the betrayal of Marshal Badoglio'. Badoglio had earlier been appointed prime minister of Italy after the king dismissed Benito Mussolini; Jerzyk's entry refers to the armistice Badoglio signed. Under the occupation, the newspaper, as one would expect, clearly had no choice but to portray the armistice as a betrayal.

4

The Urman name, according to Izydor, was originally Artman. Jews came from the westernmost part of the Hapsburg lands to the easternmost part of what would become the Austro-Hungarian Empire, to work the land as peasants and farmers. Some, including Artmans, came to a small town called Chekalufka around 1775, under Maria Theresa, Holy Roman Empress and Archduchess of Austria, after the region passed to Austria. (Rudolfs had already arrived in Kalush, some fifty years earlier). Jerzyk's grandfather, Fabian Urman, was the headmaster of the Baron de Hirsch[11] school in Tłumacz (now Tlumach), about seventy miles from Drohobycz, and close to Stanisławów. My own grandfather was briefly a Baron de Hirsch forester. Izydor gave me his copy of the *Memorial Book of Tłumacz*,[12] in English and Hebrew. The memorial book contains the photograph of the tombstone and Izydor's accompanying text (see photo section of the present publication and my comments – details in note 8). It is one of many such books commemorating murdered communities, whose remnants live in Israel and other countries. None of these communities were or could be reconstituted after the war. The town's name derives from the Turkish *tilmaç* – *tłumacz* in Polish, *tolmach* in Ukrainian and Hungarian – meaning 'translator', one of my own incarnations; apparently the town has this name either because many translators lived there or because the locals felt gratitude towards a military interpreter who dissuaded Tatars from pillaging it.

The story (perhaps apocryphal) is told of a pious, some would say too pious, rabbi in Tłumacz who, when praying, always wore white and put on two pairs of *tefilin* (phylacteries). I remember Tłumacz, a sad broken place. A typical episode from the Nazi occupation of the town: the Gestapo declared that three hundred Jews would be put to death if three men – in hiding because brave or foolhardy leaders had warned them they were on a list of wanted men – were not delivered to the SS: 'When this became known, the three at once turned themselves over to the Ukrainian militia.' That was the last that was heard of them. It is the kind of situation two poets, René Char and George Oppen, discuss in famous texts about the occupation of France.[13]

Another section of the memorial book refers to people from the town being taken to nearby Stanisławów and 'being put to death, along with hundreds of Jews, in Rudolf's Mill', which was owned by my great-uncle Samuel Rudolf before he left for Haifa around 1930; after the war it became known as Devil's Mill. However tragic and distressing the death of Jerzyk was for all concerned, he was, in the direst of situations, in command of his own destiny, unlike the poor child whose eye was gouged out, and unlike the hundreds of thousands of East Galician Jews herded into ghettos and shipped off to Bełżec and other death camps to be murdered. Such command, briefly real, is nonetheless no reward for the theft of your life.

When I finally presented Izydor with a copy of *I'm Not Even a Grown-up*, I could tell he was moved and pleased that it was out there in the world, a living component in the endless work of telling what happened to the children murdered 'over there' by 'the Nazi beast', the latter a phrase used by Jerzyk, and both phrases found in David Grossman's novel *See Under: Love* (1989).[14] I don't think Izydor read *I'm Not Even a Grown-up* – he was the last person who needed to – and I don't know how he would have reacted to what he would have understood was a betrayal of his wishes on the part of his wife. Or maybe he would have come round. This was a man who had delivered his own son and buried his own son: a rare and tragic symmetry in the life of a father. Sophie was delivered of Jerzyk and helped her husband bury him. Their life after the war, including the birth of their daughter Irit, is another story.

2011 (revised 2013 and 2016)

Notes to New Introduction (2016)

1. Emil Urman's testimony has not been translated. However, appended to it is a lengthy biographical essay and summary of his journal by Dr Raba of Yad Vashem which is included in Part III of this book, Izydor Urman's testimony. Partly written in the camp in Drohobycz where he was held before he escaped and went into hiding, and partly after the war, the testimony is more discursive and deals for the most part with topics not directly relevant to the concerns of the present book.

2. Jerzy Feliks Urman, *I'm Not Even a Grown-up: The Diary of Jerzy Feliks Urman*, edited by Anthony Rudolf. London: Menard Press/King's College, 1991.

3. Elli Wohlgelernter, 'To Smell the Jasmine: An Interview with Sophie Urman', *Jerusalem Post*, 5 November 1993. The interview marked the fiftieth anniversary of Jerzyk's death.

4. Anthony Rudolf, *Wine from Two Glasses*. 'Poetry and Politics: Trust and Mistrust in Language', lecture delivered to an invited audience at King's College, London, 17 October 1990. London: Adam Archive Publications/King's College, 1991.

5. For more details and other accounts, see www.jewishgen.org.

6. On the collaborators, see Sophie's account, pp. 66–8, and Izydor's account (pp. 85–6).

7. Jewish religious tradition counts 613 commandments in the Torah. Rabbi Emil Fackenheim (1916–2003) was a distinguished theologian.

8. I looked for the grave when I was in Drohobycz in 1991, but could not find it. The cemetery, opposite the large ruin of the great synagogue, was uncared for and probably the grave was covered over with leaves and brambles. See Plate 3 (p. 128) for a photo taken at the time. Jerzyk and other members of the family are commemorated on the tombstone of his grandmother in Bytom (see pp. 124–5 for my notes and p. 127 for the photograph). Bruno Schulz was also buried in the Drohobycz cemetery (see the eyewitness account in the long note on pp. 248–9 of *Letters and Drawings of Bruno Schulz*, edited by Jerzy Ficowski, 1988).

9. David Rubinowicz, *The Diary of David Rubinowicz*, translated by Derek Bowman. Edinburgh: William Blackwood, 1981; Éva Heyman, *The Diary of Éva Heyman*, translated by Moshe Kohn. New York: Shapolsky Publishers, 1988; Moshe Flinker, *Young Moshe's Diary*, translated by Shaul Esh. Jerusalem: Yad Vashem, 1965. As this book was going to press, I read *The Diary of Dawid Sierakowiak*, edited by Alan Adelson and translated by Kamil Turowski, New York: Oxford University Press, 1996. The last entry, from the Łódź ghetto, is 5 April 1943. Dawid, who was fifteen when the diary begins in 1939, died on 8 August 1943, about a month before

Jerzyk begins his diary. As with so many of the young people caught up in this whirlwind, Dawid's precocity and maturity – which, like the younger Jerzyk's, were forged in desperate circumstances – are evident.

10. Aryeh and Malwina Klonicki (Klonymus), *The Diary of Adam's Father, the Diary of Aryeh Klonicki (Klonymus) and His Wife Malwina, with Letters Concerning the Fate of Their Child Adam*. Tel Aviv: Ghetto Fighters House and Hakkibutz Hameuehad Publishing House, 1973.

11. See the 'Introduction to the First Edition' (p. 28) for a gloss concerning Baron de Hirsch, a remarkable individual.

    As for Jerzyk's paternal grandfather, his names, Fabian (Feivel-Shraga) Urman *hacohen*, are interesting. Grandfather Urman's given name when he was born (1873 in Austria–Hungary) was Fabian. (Latin names, e.g. Julius, were popular among Jews, including our family). Fabian's 'Hebrew' name, which all Jews have for religious purposes, was Shraga, of which a Yiddish or secular or vernacular version (*kinnui*), a 'pet' or nickname if you like, is Feivel (as so often the given name has the same first letter as the pet name, and sometimes as the Hebrew name). These names mean 'bright', 'shining', 'light'.

    I have revised a couple of Internet accounts and discussed the matter with Rabbis Howard Cooper and Frank Hellner (the latter himself a Feivel-Shraga, hence Frank) and have come up with the following: Feivish is an ancient Jewish name whose origin is the Latin *vivus* (living, alive), a loan translation or calque from the Hebrew *chaim* (life). Later, the name Feivish was considered – some say erroneously – to be a derivation from Phoebus, Greek god of the sun; consequently, Feivish (Feivel) became the *kinnui* not only for the biblical Hebrew name Uri (light) but also for the Aramaic name Shraga (candle) in the rabbinic period, presumably because a candle flame is a kind of miniature sun. So, Fabian's 'Hebrew' name was unusually an Aramaic name (paradoxically Aramaic itself was the vernacular of the day). The word '*shraga*' is often found in the Talmud. Most often, a Hebrew name really is a Hebrew name.

    In addition, we know from the photograph of the family grave with the accompanying commentary by Izydor that Fabian was *hacohen* (the *cohen* or priest). Since the family name was not Cohen there must have been an ancient family tradition passed from father to son across the centuries that they were Cohens, descendants of the older brother of Moses: Aaron, the first High Priest. Since Fabian was a Cohen, so were Izydor and Jerzyk. Recent research has shown that even now Ashkenazi and Sephardi Cohens have a similar DNA profile, which therefore antedates the Diaspora. In the wrong hands, this could create problems on the Temple Mount one day but I am straying from our theme.

12. Shlomo Bond et al. (eds), *Memorial Book of Tłumacz*, translated by Yocheved Klausner. Tel Aviv: Tłumacz Society, 1976. Available at http://www.jewishgen.org/yizkor/tlumacz/tlumacz.html.

The original photograph of the tombstone can be found on p. 494 of the memorial book and is reproduced here as Plate 1).

13. René Char, *Feuillets d'Hypnos (1973)*, translated by Mark Hutchinson and entitled *Hypnos*. London/New York/Calcutta: Seagull Books, 2014; George Oppen, 'Route', in Michael Davidson (ed.), *New Collected Poems*. New York: New Directions, 2008, pp. 192–202.

14. David Grossman, *See Under: Love*, translated by Betsy Rosenberg. London: Jonathan Cape, 1990. 'I can most highly recommend the Gestapo to everyone,' wrote Sigmund Freud in 1938 on being permitted finally to leave Vienna, at which point he was ordered by the Germans to say he had been treated correctly. Sarcasm as defiance, and, in such circumstances, risky defiance.

Revised Final Section of Introduction to the First Edition (1991)
(with New Glosses in Italics)

There are a number of problems concerning the text which so far remain unresolved because I have not been able to consult the original manuscript, which seems to be missing, for reasons that are not yet clear. [*See New Introduction.*] I have worked from a photocopy of an authentic transcript made by Jerzyk's Uncle Emil after the war. According to a note by a Yad Vashem researcher, 'After what Jerzyk experienced he uses only initials and often breaks off a word in the middle. Many years later Emil filled in the gaps while going through the diary during a grave illness.' Emil died in Israel in 1956. I cannot always identify these insertions from the transcript. Nor can I check my belief that some of the parentheses in the transcript were added by Emil to explain obscurities. I have indicated these in notes. [*These annotations in parentheses were indeed by Emil. The notes to Jerzyk's diary have accordingly been amended.*]

After the entry of 13 September there is a row of asterisks and then no entry till 24 October. I believe there may be some missing entries, especially as the chronological part of the diary (see below) is headed 'From the diary'. Attached to Izydor's own short testimony are some diary fragments by Jerzyk which I have appended after the diary. [*See the introductory comment to section 'Notes to the Diary and Diary Fragments of Jerzy Feliks Urman'.*] After the first four, the remaining twenty-eight cover the missing period. This could mean either that the full entries are missing or that for unknown reasons he stopped doing the diary during this period. If the manuscript turns up one day some of these mysteries may be resolved. [*It is now clear from the original manuscript studied by Antonia Lloyd-Jones and myself that there are no missing entries and that this period is covered – the dates fit – by the diary notes, which we have renamed 'fragments' to avoid confusion with actual notes. It seems likely that Jerzyk intended to write them up. But the state of the manuscript is indicative of the situation the family found themselves in and the state of mind the boy was in.*]

Finally, there is the problem of dates in two entries. Beginning with the third entry, the diary [*–in a green, lined school notebook, bound and loose sheets–*] is chronological, that is, 10 September till 12 November. Two entries are [*in a separate square-ruled school notebook with a pink cover*] dated 27 and 28 October, the month in figures and therefore perhaps easier to get wrong accidentally than a spelt-out word. However, there are also entries under 27 and 28 October in the green diary. It is just possible they were misdated and written on 27 and 28 August. They deal chronologically with earlier events, beginning with the German invasion of the Soviet Union's Polish eastern territories in June 1941 They do not touch on day-to-day life in hiding. They are very different in character, tone, and style from the main diary. But he could have written these entries in October as a kind of introduction to the diary proper, without the help of Uncle Emil, as Jerzyk says, but doubtless with his encouragement. [*After examining the original documents, Antonia Lloyd-Jones and I are certain that Jerzyk wrote the two entries on the given dates rather than carelessly misdate them without anyone noticing and correcting later. Written sixteen days before he died, they read like the start of a never-to-be-completed narrative of the period before they were in hiding – see note 9 in section 'Notes to the Diary and Diary Fragments of Jerzy Feliks Urman' for a clue – quite separate from the day-to-day account of their life in hiding as found in the main diary in the 'Green Notebook'.*]

Introduction to the First Edition (1991)
(with Slight Changes and Updates, and Without the Final Section)

1

Jerzy Feliks Urman (Jerzyk) was born on 9 April 1932 in the East Galician town of Stanisławów, as it was known between the two world wars when it was under Polish rule. The town was part of Poland–Lithuania until 1772, and then Austria–Hungary (with a brief break when it was part of the Russian Empire) till 1918 during which time it was called Stanislau. From the end of the Second World War until Ukraine became independent in 1991, the region was part of the Soviet Union and was known as West Ukraine. In the early years of Soviet rule it was called Stanislav until 1962, when it was renamed Ivano-Frankovsk – not that you would know from the *Wikipedia* article on the town – then, on independence, Ivano-Frankivsk. The year before Jerzyk was born, Jews formed over forty per cent of the town's total population of fifty thousand; by the beginning of the war the proportion was nearer fifty per cent. In 1939, one million two hundred thousand or ten per cent of the East Galician population was Jewish, to which were added three hundred thousand refugees by 1941.

Ivano-Frankivsk is close to Tysmenytsia (before the war, Tyśmienica), birthplace of Freud's father, to Drohobych (Drohobycz), the town of the writer Bruno Schulz, and to Czernowitz (now Chernivtsi), birthplace of the poet Paul Celan. As Stanislau, the town was the birthplace in 1893 of Daniel Auster, the first mayor of Jerusalem and a relative of the author Paul Auster.[1] East Galicia (as well as Volhynia and Podolia to the east in the Pale of Settlement) was one of the heartlands of Hasidism and *shtetl* life. Jerzyk's paternal grandfather, Fabian Urman, was headmaster of the Baron de Hirsch school in Tłumacz (now Tlumach). (De Hirsch was one of the greatest Jewish philanthropists of all time. Among his main concerns were education of Jews in impoverished Galicia and emigration from Russia to the United States and Argentina, for the purposes of agricultural resettlement.)

The nearest big town to Stanisławów was Lwów, previously Lemberg and, later, Lvov and Lviv (see previous mention of geo-historical changes). Jerzyk's father Izydor became a doctor specialising in obstetrics and gynaecology after studies at Lwów and Vienna universities. Jerzyk's uncle Emil taught in the Faculty of Law at Lwów University. His other paternal uncle, Artur, was a leading petroleum engineer in Drohobycz and managing director of the 'Galicia' refinery. Thus Jerzyk was born into the professional classes, the intelligentsia, of East Galicia. The language of the home was Polish, but Yiddish was spoken and understood and Hebrew was studied for religious purposes. Between the wars there were fifty-five synagogues in the town. Today there is one. Jewish life survives there for the time being, thanks to a teacher and *tsaddik* (righteous man), Viktor Kolesnik. The several hundred Jews are almost all from elsewhere, given that the few survivors understandably emigrated, mainly to Israel and the United States.

The forebears of the Urmans arrived in the nearby village of Chekalufka as part of a drive by the authorities in Vienna to colonise and 'Germanise' the eastern lands with Jews. Jerzyk's maternal grandparents, the Arbeits, left for Palestine in 1930 and settled in Petah Tikva. He and his parents even visited them in 1935. My grandfather, Joseph Rudolf, Izydor's first cousin, left Stanisławów for England via Hungary, intending to move on to America, in 1903, and that – which is another story – is why I am in a position to tell *this* story, the story of Jerzy Feliks Urman, who died at the age of eleven, a victim of the Final Solution.

The Soviet Union occupied Poland's eastern territories including East Galicia in September 1939, in accordance with the secret terms of the Nazi–Soviet Pact agreed in August. Stanisławów itself was occupied on 18 September. Poland was partitioned on 28 September. The western part was incorporated into the Reich. What remained was governed by Germany under the so-called General Government. By and large, the Jews of the eastern territories welcomed the Red Army. Germany declared war on the Soviet Union on 22 June 1941: Operation Barbarossa. Within a few weeks the region was overrun. Stanisławów province was incorporated into the General Government. In May the term 'Final Solution' had been used in an official document for the first time. Readers are referred to the late Martin Gilbert's brilliantly organised spatio-temporal account in *The Holocaust* (1987) of the implementation of the Final Solution. As already stated in my new introduction, East Galicia, Jerzyk's homeland, hosted more enthusiastic collaboration by the local population (against Jews and also Poles) than anywhere else in Europe, the killing fields well and truly ploughed by the Einsatzgruppen and their local teams in the wake of the Wehrmacht. It is the region where many of the cruellest *Aktionen* and most sadistic killings took place, even by the high standards set by the Nazis. Reuben Ainsztein's *Jewish Resistance in Nazi-occupied Eastern Europe*, a book neglected for political and other reasons when it came out in 1974, but properly praised by Gilbert, reveals how Jews faced, and where possible resisted, Ukrainian nationalists as well as the occupying Germans. Among the Ukrainians, says Ainsztein, 'the only friends of the Jews were the Baptist peasants, a few noble individuals belonging to the minute liberal intelligentsia, and a few surviving Socialists and Communists'.[2] Evidence from the Soviet archives paints an even blacker picture of collaboration than we thought. This was not fertile ground for traditional modes of resistance, though every documented case can be found in Ainsztein's book.

At least six hundred intellectuals and professionals were murdered in Stanisławów on 3 August 1941; and then, on the Jewish festival of Hoshana Rabbah, during the night of 12 October, ten thousand Jews were murdered in an *Aktion* in the cemetery. On 15 December the Stanisławów ghetto was set up. Things deteriorated further in 1942. There were more *Aktionen*. Part of the ghetto was set on fire in March. Jewish leaders were left hanging from lamp posts for a week. Five thousand Jews were deported to Bełżec at the beginning of April; some of them were marched to the station on their knees. They included a thousand Hungarian Jews who had been incarcerated in 'Rudolf's Mill'. [*See New Introduction.*] On the first day of the Jewish New Year, 12 September 1942, five thousand more Jews were deported to Bełżec, including Jerzyk's paternal grandfather, Fabian Urman. The next day, in London, the editor was eight days old…

By the end of 1942, surviving *shtetl* Jews from hundreds of villages and small towns in East Galicia were concentrated in a small number of ghettos. Early in 1943 the remainder of the Stanisławów community was murdered in the cemetery and Stanisławów became the first town in East Galicia to be '*Judenfrei*'. Jews had lived there continuously since 1662, the heyday of Shabbetai Zvi, and not long after the Chmielnicki massacres.

2

One day in 1942, probably between April and August, in the Stanisławów ghetto, Jerzyk had returned home trembling. He told his parents what he had witnessed on a ghetto street: a German caught a little boy who had been smuggling food into the ghetto. The German gouged out the child's eye with a red-hot wire: 'The eye was dangling on the wire.' Without any shadow of doubt this terrible episode in the life of an unknown child (whose memorial too this book is) contributed decisively to the manner of Jerzyk's own death.

After witnessing this characteristically sadistic action on the part of the SS, Jerzyk, already precocious, suddenly grew up. His parents must have realised he understood everything. Up to that point they would have tried to protect him from the terrible reality on the streets and in their hearts; he, perhaps, would have derived comfort from the thought that all of them might survive and reach the Yishuv in Palestine after the war. Earlier, among his many projects, he had made elaborate plans for growing mushrooms in hothouses in Palestine on a large scale. According to his uncle Emil he had worked on schemes to save the Jewish people and all humanity.

'I won't go without cyanide,' he said when the family was discussing the possibility of leaving the ghetto. 'I will never let them take me alive.' Izydor had a supply of the poison, a much-prized possession, obtainable at a price on the black market.[3] They agreed they would survive together or die together. They would not allow themselves to be tortured and deported; Jerzyk was afraid he would give names and hiding places away under torture, as his mother Sophie says in her memoir. There you will find her descriptions of his death and of its aftermath.

By October 1942 Izydor knew he must not delay his decision to organise a hiding place for his family. Thanks to his brother Artur in Drohobycz, there was a chance this could succeed. Artur sent a trusted female employee, Mrs Rudnicka, to collect Jerzyk from Stanisławów and hide him with a Polish family outside the Drohobycz ghetto. That month two thousand Jews were deported to Bełżec from the ghetto. In Drohobycz Bruno Schulz had less than a month to live.[4] In November another employee came to fetch Sophie and bring her to a hiding place. Like Jerzyk she had, of course, to leave the Stanisławów ghetto without permission. After a few days spent hiding outside the ghetto, she arrived in Drohobycz. Artur, along with other professionals, was living in a special camp in the 'Galicia' refinery. Sophie was brought to Jerzyk's hiding place, the house of Mrs Huczyńska, whose son had taken Sophie from Stanisławów. That night Artur brought some food, a fake identification (ID) card for Sophie and an *Arbeitskarte*, confirmation that she was working as a technical designer at his plant. Sophie's appearance was sufficiently 'Aryan' to enable her to pass as a Polish Catholic woman, though of course this remained extremely risky since she might be recognised or her 'disguise' seen through. The *Arbeitskarte* was signed by Artur's boss, a colonel in the German army and an engineer in civilian life. He and Artur got on well. Artur explained that Sophie was his Polish girlfriend. After about three days, three members of the local militia with a dog searched the house where Sophie and Jerzyk were hiding but somehow failed to trace them. The Gestapo had arrested the landlady's two grown-up sons earlier. Distraught, she asked Sophie and Jerzyk to leave.

Late December on the edge of town. They obviously could not head for the centre and therefore set off through the snowy fields. After about an hour Jerzyk was tired and wanted to lie down and sleep. Sophie resisted this mortally dangerous idea. They wandered all night. Next morning, with no alternative, they returned to the house. The landlady begged forgiveness. She gave them tea and bread and asked them to pray to Saint Mary who had saved them. Every month Sophie had to renew her *Arbeitskarte* at the residence of Artur's boss, Colonel V. B. He and his beautiful blonde secretary were kind and helpful.[5] Shortly afterwards, Izydor was collected from Stanisławów during a snowstorm, on a farm truck sent by Artur. The truck was stopped by two Germans; the driver's hand shook but he showed them forged papers. Izydor had some gold coins in a silver cigarette box, but he threw them out of the window in case they were searched. On his arrival, the family moved to another hiding place.

By March 1943, Jerzyk, his parents, his paternal grandmother, and (from September, see p. 110) his uncle Emil were in hiding in the apartment of Artur's former housekeeper, Hela, on 10 Górna Brama Street. In the other apartment of the same house lived two Polish women, Marysia and Genia. Jerzyk's diary and Sophie's memoir tell what happened in the last few months of his life.

Here is Izydor's own account of Jerzyk's death: 'The Kripos[6] came in. Now we knew Marysia and Genia sent our murderers. They spoke Polish. "You are Jews." "No we're not." One of them hit me behind the ear with the butt of his pistol. I fell, covered with blood. Jerzyk immediately put the poison in his mouth. "Daddy, cyan…", and he fell to the floor. They were shocked and left.' Without killing or removing or even reporting the parents.

Overall, Jerzyk had been in hiding for more than a year by the time he died. He was little more than eleven and a half years old when he committed suicide. But even if one makes allowances for his age and for the terrible stresses and strains attendant upon being cooped up in one room for that length of time in those circumstances (see Sophie's diary; Jerzyk's own diary shows he knew about executions, round-ups, etc., and of course he had not forgotten the ghetto episode involving the child), even if one makes those allowances and accepts the consequential possibility that he judged the situation wrongly (Sophie describes the demand for money when the police returned after Jerzyk's death and it was Emil's view later that the first visit was for blackmail or ransom purposes), even so, the event under description suggests the likelihood that he was in command of his destiny. It suggests that this was resistance of the noblest and most tragic kind, just as the keeping of the diary must be accounted a form of non-violent resistance.[7] As I have said, Ukrainian, and to a lesser extent Polish, complicity in Nazi crimes in East Galicia made traditional concepts of armed resistance much more difficult, and often impossible.

Izydor was present when Sophie gave birth to Jerzyk; indeed, he delivered him. And then they buried their son in the backyard with their own hands, later reburying him in the local cemetery. To bury your own son is rare enough (certainly in the Western world), to deliver him even rarer, to do both may be unique, and unbearably so. The parents believe the son's death saved their lives. This is a burden. They chose to live. This too counts as resistance. Their daughter Irit was born after the war in Bytom, Silesia, in 1945. They left Poland for France and went to Israel in 1949.

Jerzyk is my second cousin once removed. His father, Izydor, was my late paternal grandfather's first cousin, their mothers Rosie and Hermina Vogel being sisters or more likely half sisters, since Hermina was twenty two years younger than Rosie. I learnt about Jerzyk's fate when researching what happened to those members of my grandfather's family who did not emigrate to Palestine or America or England in time to avoid the German occupation and its consequences. I discussed the traumatic events with Izydor and Sophie several times; you do not need to have seen Claude Lanzmann's film *Shoah* (1985) to know what pain such excavating brings to the surface. One visit was in April 1991, shortly before a long desired pilgrimage to Stanisławów and Drohobycz. I wanted to clarify certain obscurities and problems in the diary. On and off, for many years, I had worked in, on, and around the 'subject', making notes, drafting poems, reading books, comparing testimonies, attending lectures, etc. My regular visits to Israel always included seeing the Urmans and also researching in the Yad Vashem archives in Jerusalem, which supplied me with a photocopy of Emil's transcription of Jerzyk's diary (and other documents including Izydor's testimony) many years earlier. On the plane and in buses I read James Young's recent and crucial book *Writing and Rewriting the Holocaust* (1990). He would be the first to agree that one should not become obsessed by self-conscious anxiety about formal categories and genres, about theories of documentary versus poetry, and so on.[8] Above all one must respect the over-there-ness, the otherness of the material and one must reflect on all the meanings of the word obliquity. It is a terrible privilege to publish the diary, a *mitzvah*, an obligation. Jerzyk himself wanted it to be published, even though, in his own words, 'I'm not a professional writer. I'm not even a grown-up.'

The boy spent eight months in one room in 10 Górna Brama Street in Drohobycz. Sophie drew a plan for me, Volodya Tsimberg of Lvov drove me there, and we were shown around the town by Alfred Schreier, a former student of Bruno Schulz. First we saw the various places associated with this writer of genius, and then we drove to Górna Brama Street.

We go into the backyard. A small shed is in the right place. 'Is it the original barn where Sophie and Izydor buried Jerzyk?' 'No. It was built after the war.' The well is no longer there. A Ukrainian woman gives us permission to come inside. On our left is the apartment of Marysia and Genia, who betrayed them. On our right Hela's place, Hela the former housekeeper of Artur Urman. She hid them for money and perhaps out of religious obligation. This is her room which was (and still is) a kitchen. Then into the next room, with the woman's daughter attentive and understanding. In this room Jerzyk died, one of a million and a half children murdered in a genocide whose cruelty and cowardice all readers of this diary are aware of.

We go into the third room, where his grandmother Hermina and Uncle Emil hid. I take my photographs. It is time to return to Lvov. In the car I realise that I failed to say Kaddish for Jerzyk in his room. This will be remedied in the Stanisławów cemetery, where our mutual relative, my great grandmother Rosa Vogel Rudolf is buried. Czesław Miłosz talks of the pressure of history on experience. In Jerzyk's case both were extreme. Had Jerzyk not killed himself, what would have happened? Perhaps they would all have been murdered in Drohobycz or been deported to Bełżec at once or to Auschwitz later. But, most likely, before then they would all have swallowed the cyanide, as agreed. Or they might all have survived, as indeed the four adults did. Perhaps Jerzyk's death did save them, as his parents believe. This is one aspect of a burden no one should have to bear. And we should not dwell on it, except to say that given the events described earlier it is as certain as anything can be that Jerzyk was entitled to have cyanide and his parents were right to allow him to keep it on him. And this on one level is all we need to know about the Nazis.

Jerzyk died by his own hand on 13 November 1943. He was not yet twelve years old. His diary cannot be compared with the major published testimonies of children, such as those by Anne Frank, Moshe Flinker, Eva Heyman, David Rubinowicz, and Dawid Sierakowiak. For one thing it is too short and too fragmentary. There is not sufficient accumulated detail to enable one to construct an analysis of the diarist's situation and attitude as one could with the others – four of whom died in concentration camps. Even so, I believe publication is more than an act of piety or posthumous defiance. The circumstances of his tragic death speak for themselves, with the help of Sophie's two accounts. And there is a great deal of interest in the diary, in terms of movement and displacement, threat and rumour, nervous energy and fear, pain and insight. Intellectual and cultural activities in the Warsaw Ghetto and elsewhere were a form of spiritual resistance, an assertion of humanity against the Nazi definition and treatment of Jews as non-human. Jerzyk could keep a diary. To stay alive as a moral sentient human being (and this includes rational suicide) may in a vortex of evil be the only form of resistance possible. The desperate purity of his act shocks and, dare I say, inspires us even now – on condition we honour him by working to prevent such situations from ever needing to happen again. This will keep us busy till the end of days.

Notes to Introduction to the First Edition (1991)

1. Paul Auster's family were close neighbours of the family of another relative of mine, Bronka Vogel Fliderbaum (a first cousin of Izydor's), a fact Auster alludes to in his book *The Invention of Solitude* (1982), where he recounts discussing our families with me. [*Details of this and other books in this introduction can be found in the Select Bibliography.*]

2. While this savage indictment is hardly an exaggeration, Ainzstein should have referred to Metropolitan Archbishop Andrei Sheptytsky, the head of the Ukrainian church who 'issued a pastoral letter "Thou shalt not murder" and took the audacious step of addressing a letter to Heinrich Himmler protesting the extermination. No other ecclesiastical figure of equal rank in the whole of Europe displayed such sorrow for the fate of the Jews and acted so boldly on their behalf.' He was not the only member of his church to act in this way. The quote is from Erich Goldhagen's introduction to Rabbi David Kahane's *Lvov Ghetto Diary* (1990, p. 441). Kahane, his wife, and daughter all survived under the protection of the Archbishop. Overall, Kahane confirms Ainsztein's view.

3. See Piotr Rawicz's *Blood from the Sky* (1981) and Kahane's *Lvov Ghetto Diary* (1990) for conflicting accounts of the poison's availability. Robert Marshall, in *In the Sewers of Lvov* (1990), says this was one black market trade that the Germans did nothing to curtail.

4. For the only eyewitness account of his death, see *Letters and Drawings of Bruno Schulz*, edited by Jerzy Ficowski (1988, pp. 248–9).

5. Some months later, on the last occasion when Sophie went to have her card renewed, Colonel V. B. had gone, doubtless fleeing at the news of the impending arrival of the Red Army (7 August 1944). Izydor began working again as a doctor, Sophie as a nurse. One day the secretary called out to her in the street. They chatted. She admitted that she too was Jewish. V. B. had saved her life. He knew that Sophie too was Jewish but didn't let on, to make her feel more secure. After the war Sophie traced his address, but he never answered her letter. [*2015: Sadly, it never occurred to me to attempt to track him down twenty-five years ago, when he could still have been alive.*]

6. Shorthand slang for *Kriminal Polizei*, local militia collaborating with the Germans. Izydor thinks they were Silesians. Perhaps they were ethnic Germans.

7. In a major scholarly study, *Children with a Star* (1991), Deborah Dwork writes about the lives of the children, both the one and a half million who died and the eleven per cent of the 1939 population who survived. Many of the children kept diaries. One of her themes concerns the women who were not doing 'men's work' (i.e. armed resistance), and their neglect in the literature. She draws attention to the work of those women in the Jewish resistance who protected and succoured those in hiding and on

the run, especially children. Perhaps understandably she is a little unfair to Reuben Ainsztein. But at the time that he was writing *Jewish Resistance in Nazi-occupied Eastern Europe*, such resistance was neglected or ignored in conventional historiography ('they went like lambs . . .', etc.); his documentary celebration of this activity makes his book crucially important and he should be honoured as a pioneer. Nearly twenty years later Dwork brought another and complementary world view to this territory, as did Lawrence Langer in *Holocaust Testimonies* (1991) – compare his earlier work in a more traditional conceptual framework – although Langer's later book is marred by a personalised attack on Martin Gilbert.

8. I have discussed these matters in two earlier texts: in *At an Uncertain Hour* (1990) and in my 1990 Adam Lecture at King's College, London, published as *Wine from Two Glasses* (1991), as well as in two later texts: *Engraved in Flesh* (1996; revised edition, 2007) and my 2001 Pierre Rouve Memorial Lecture in *Rescue Work: Memory and Text*, published in *Stand* 5(3), 2004. The long bibliographies appended to these four texts complement the somewhat shorter ones included in the present volume.

PART II

The Diary of (and Other Texts by)
Sophie Urman
with Introduction and Notes

Introduction to the Diary
of (and Other Texts by) Sophie Urman

Sophie (née Arbeit) Urman was born in East Galicia (West Ukraine) in 1911, when it was still a province of Austria–Hungary. It was Poland between the two world wars, and Polish was her first language. She married Izydor Urman (Miki) in the Hotel Bristol in Lwów on Sunday, 30 December 1930. The couple lived in Stanisławów, where their son Jerzyk was born in 1932. Sophie begins her diary a few weeks after Jerzyk died in the tragic circumstances already explained. I have glossed the entries as best I can with the expert advice of Antonia Lloyd-Jones. The notes are obligatory for the editor of such a text and essential for the historical record, but the reader can decide as he/she goes along whether to consult or skip them. Sophie made twenty-seven entries, around the same number as in Jerzyk's main diary, but each of them is usually much longer than his.

The diary fits into a green-covered school exercise book, with pages to spare. Sophie's entries were written over a period of seven months and stop mid-entry with the arrival of the Russians and an end to the war in that part of Europe. Although, as is clear from his diary, Jerzyk was precocious and intelligent and thoughtful, he was not a grown-up (as he himself says), whereas his mother was thirty-three when the boy died, seven years younger than her husband; she followed the war as closely as possible in the circumstances. Unlike her husband, she did not 'look Jewish' and passed as a Christian Pole, which meant she could leave the house, with all the very different complications and risks that this entailed, such as behaving like a pious Christian in church. Privately, she was quite religious as a Jewess and said her prayers regularly (see diary entry 6.II.1944, pp. 44–5), even speaking them under her breath in church. She did secretarial work in the refinery, and later worked as a nurse.

It has not always been possible to identify people whose names are only given as initials, or even full names. I have to take responsibility for not asking enough questions when it was still possible. By the time I realised, it was too late. This is frustrating but it does involve one even more in the secrecy and precautions and frustrations of the diary keepers. Sophie's diary is intelligent, observant, and understandably outspoken. The most striking impression is of someone determined – after initial and understandable hesitation – to survive, partly in spite of, partly because of the death of the child. Her daughter Irit was born in Bytom in southern Poland on 29 October 1945, which means she was conceived in Drohobycz around the time of the liberation of Auschwitz at the end of January 1945.

In the diary entry of 27 December 1943, Sophie discusses the question of whether to move again. She and her husband moved earlier in December, she, as before, living openly, her husband having to remain in hiding in the attic, leaving her mother-in-law (and probably her brother-in-law) hidden in 10 Górna Brama Street, where Jerzyk had been buried behind the house. On 13 January, two months after Jerzyk killed himself, she apostrophises her son. On 28 January, she reflects on the Soviet Union's local battles with Nazi Germany and also, again, about the possibility of moving to another place. And she addresses Jerzyk again. On 6 February, she writes more about the Russian advances, and Jerzyk is addressed as her baby. She asks herself whether they too should have killed themselves and suggests that his death, his noble sacrifice, saved them. In the newspaper interview forty years later, she discusses her husband's feelings of guilt about their (or his) agreement that the boy would be allowed to keep his own cyanide but, as I explain (p. 19), Jerzyk would not have gone into hiding without it. Her interview discusses the impact on some readers of the publication of Jerzyk's diary and their mistaken sense that his parents were responsible for Jerzyk's death.

13 May: the first entry for more than three months, is an anniversary entry, written six months after the boy's death. In it she writes about his being on all fours in the garden – quoted in her article (see p. 66) – and around here the diary page is smudged, we may suppose with her tears. After this long entry, there are seven blank pages followed by an entry in pencil on 1 June (continuing in pencil for two entries and part of a third), which was in fact 2 June (see note for that date *et seq.*). Here, again, Sophie addresses her son. On 4 June (i.e. 5) she discusses the fighting, and on 5 June (i.e. 6) she makes a clear reference to D-Day. On 6 June (i.e. 7), she quotes a sentence, relevant to her situation, from the work of a popular, insignificant, and now forgotten Polish writer. The next day there is more about the fighting in France and the following day she quotes a very ordinary German poem (translated in the notes), again directly relevant to her situation. And so what if these texts are ordinary?: 'Millions in their bereavements, heartbreaks, agonies, depressions, have been comforted and perhaps saved from despair by appalling trash while poetry stood helplessly and incompetently by' (W. H. Auden, 'Squares and Oblongs', 1948). Next, there are two short entries and then, on 13 June (i.e. 14), she again addresses her son, seven months after his death. The next entry is a fascinating description of a street encounter with a Gestapo man, followed by one short entry before we reach 23 June, when she discusses the V-bomb attacks on London. If I may anticipate the relevant note: here the story of Jerzyk poignantly intersects with that of my London cousin Mark Rothstein, killed by a V-2 missile on 27 March 1945, the final day of these attacks. I have included my account of his life and death (Mark and Jerzyk

are both related to me but not to each other) as an appendix to this book. On Friday, 7 July, Sophie discusses day-to-day life and the progress of the war.

A very short entry follows and then, on Monday, 23 July, there is more about the fighting; she reports a rumour: 'The Ukrainians are going to attack the Poles.' On 24 July, she describes front-line German troops heading for Sambor, some of them barefoot: 'They look like an army on the retreat.' The Russians were encouraging German troops to surrender, and then there is an entry about fighting. She addresses her dead son again. The following entry finds Sophie in church. On Friday, 4 August, she reports Russian bombing of the town and in the final entry, on 6 August, she tells her son that the Russians have finally arrived in Drohobycz.

Sophie's carefully composed article (originally for an English language class), which follows the diary, tells of their experiences in the Stanisławów ghetto – note their correct instinct to flee – and Jerzyk's reburial in August in the Jewish cemetery in Drohobycz and what happened at the liberation. At the time of writing, I am still making enquiries, but I fear the grave is no longer there. Note too her remarks about moving with her husband from the house where they had been in hiding with Jerzyk, her mother-in-law, and her brother-in-law, Emil. No mention is made of her brother-in-law but the evidence from Jerzyk's diary suggests he was in Drohobycz, returning after an attempt to escape to Hungary. Earlier in the year he had been in a forced-labour camp in Drohobycz, but must have escaped.

'May the Blood': The Diary of Sophie Urman

Translated by Antonia Lloyd-Jones

The Christmas holidays went by peacefully. We were expecting H.'s brother[1] but he didn't come. It turned out he had in fact received a pass, but in Sambor he found out that people were being hanged here,[2] in view of which he returned home. Next day I paid a visit to pU.[3] where I stopped a little longer than planned, causing everyone at home to get upset, and Miki[4] even reproached me.[5]

27.XII.1943

The question of the *syrenka*.[6] I've already been to see S.[7] about this. He promised that perhaps it can be arranged. On the other hand, [*N.? or H.?*][8] promised something, perhaps through her relative, but he[9] said that for now there's no hurry, and that there are several similar matters on the go. We'll see.

More important for the moment would be the question of a change of accommodation. Until now it has not been possible to try get a place because of the lack of furniture and for all sorts of other reasons. Now I might be lent one in which I've lived before. To this end, as soon as the holiday is over, I'll go and make a definitive attempt to get an apartment I've had my eye on for a long time now. I'm not claiming it'll be any better, or more comfortable either, but perhaps with some far-reaching caution at least I might succeed. I'd like to be a little more independent and not so constantly reliant on the changeable whims and moods of [*T.?*][10] whom one might define as '*die Kraft, die Gutes will und Böses schafft*'. [*'The power which desires good manages to do evil'*.][11]

13.I.1944

My one and only Son! Two months have passed since that terrible day when evil people caused your death. Here I am writing that word, though I still can't believe it. Sometimes it feels as if you're just absent for a while, and sometimes I try to convince myself that we've hidden you in a safe place, to protect you from the degradation and atrocities of this incredible war until it's over. Surely since the world began, there can never have been such a terrible disaster, devised by such Satanic minds. Dear Son, Mother Earth has proved extremely merciful. She clasps everyone to her bosom, rich and poor alike, the poorest and the richest, people of any denomination and nationality, and is not governed by the cruel laws invented by our assassins, which hold that only people of *ar*[12] origin are allowed to walk on her surface, whatever their worth or ability, to render service to anyone else in life. My dear Son, now you've gone to another mother, surely more worthy of such a treasure than I, who failed to protect you. I envy her for hiding so many children in her bosom, but my little Kitten, you were all I had, and now I'm on my own. I no longer visit you twice a day as I used to, because I'm afraid to attract the attention of the *klemp*.[13] I only say 'Good morning', and 'Good night', once, on Fridays before bed.[14] Every time Daddy has tears in his eyes, because he's reminded of home and all the happy times we spent together. Who could have foreseen that we were destined for such a terrible homelessness, and that such a painful blow lay ahead of us! I'm perfectly aware that we're not the only ones, but for us that's poor consolation.

28.I.1944, Friday

I haven't written for a terribly long time now. This idleness really is unforgivable, because in the meantime all sorts of interesting things have happened. Above all the winter attack by the Bolsheviks has ~~reached~~[15] grown to a large scale. They have pushed forward on almost the entire front, changing the offensive now in one, now in another place. Apparently they've even crossed the (former) Polish border near Sam.[16] There has been close fighting there, and it's still going on. Much alarm, above all among the Ukrainians and Volksdeutsch.[17] The Germans are trying not to show alarm, but perhaps they're feeling very strong. Some people, fearing an evacuation (in my view prematurely), are packing up, determined to leave for the west. I don't know by what means they intend to carry out their plans, because since November 1943 the railway has been inaccessible to the civilian population of non-German origin. Besides, as far as I know, without the permission of the authorities no one is allowed to move from place to place unless they have an important reason.

For the time being, all the trouble on the streets has calmed down. The Bolsheviks have been driven back, to outside Zaszków and near Pohre-byszcze, and now the point of gravity lies in the environs of Leningrad and Lake Ilmen, and thus to the far north. People have already stopped talking about running away, and personally I think that before the spring absolutely no change is likely to take place on our territory.

Two weeks ago [*Szaszka?*][18] went on an expedition. She didn't find the shelter very satisfying, she spent one 24-hour period there, the rest of the week at the owner's place, and came home. I don't think she's suited to such escapades (she's too keen on comfort), and besides she may possibly be right to suggest that for the time being there's no need.

I saw S., and he categorically refused me the *syrenka*, but I haven't the strength to get upset about it, maybe the Lord God will make everything work out all right. I'll try a different way.

So far I haven't found a flat. People are reluctant to rent out, because the prices are low (36–40 złoty for a room with a kitchen) so they'd rather leave the flats empty than have the bother of lodgers. Nevertheless I keep trying, and have even asked Mrs [R.?][19] to intervene. She promised to help as much as possible. Apart from that I gave her the shining bird to sell, a keepsake I was given by my Mother, when I gave birth to you, my little Son. I wouldn't sell it, but we need the money, and when it gets a bit hotter I don't know if I'll be able to turn it into cash.

H. brought news a commission from Lwów came to the factory: an announcement was made that all 'Jews' can work in peace to the end of the war and needn't run away, because an order has come from Berlin forbidding their killing.

Miki and I were both deeply moved – one simply refuses to believe this evil could possibly be coming to an end. Nevertheless, I don't believe it, because assurances of this kind have been made before. Nevertheless[20] it's a pity, dear Jerzyk, you didn't live through to this moment. You would be happy as usual, you'd raise your little arms and thank the Lord God, and you'd even clap with delight. How desperate it is that I must keep thinking of you as something past and gone and live only on memories, imagining what you would have done in this or another situation. Now for a change the situation has grown worse again, things are happening somewhere, but we don't know exactly what, because the newspapers either don't mention them or bring belated news. A few days ago I read an announcement condemning 20 Ukrainians to death for belonging to a nationalist party, and for helping partisans, and a housemaid was executed too for supporting the Jews. The sentence was carried out on the 10th at Stryj, and the rest were pardoned.

There's new trouble with the gas. A notice came from the gasworks to say that a regulator has to be fitted by 1 February, otherwise they'll cut off the gas. We know the price of a regulator (about 550 złoty), but we don't yet know where to get it.

6.II.1944

The regulator has been sorted out. The neighbours dealt with the matter to mutual satisfaction. The price is of course much higher, but they believe this will make up for the missing parts of the gas stove; what's more, they're proud they've managed to sort something out. And I'm pleased I didn't have to deal with it all. I try to be diplomatic with them, as long as I don't run into obstacles provided by H. of course. She's quite capable in her crudeness and naivety of ruining everything at a single blow, which I don't find remotely amusing, because I haven't the strength for domestic squabbles, on top of the stress we're permanently under anyway.

The situation is getting better and better. The B.[21] are moving forward, 2 days ago they took Łuck and Równe. I realise that the war won't be over any time soon, but I'm very much hoping for at least a little freedom for M., who's trapped like a prisoner without any air. As long as you were here, my darling little Baby, you filled his time with your presence and your constant prattle, but now it has all gone so quiet ... Only Szaszka hawks loudly now and then, which is even more upsetting.

Yesterday H. came by to say that someone there took [*blank space*][22] at your place. You can imagine what effect that had on me. I keep asking God at least to guarantee peace for your poor little soul, since it wasn't granted to you in life. I am coming round to the fact, my dear, my only Child, that you fell victim to reprehensible, criminal people and your noble sacrifice was the only thing that saved us. We're not worthy of it, dear little Son, and I don't know if we should have accepted it, or should instead have obeyed the first impulses of emotion and followed after you. We were definitely not worthy of you. We walk about, we eat, drink and read – in short we vegetate, for you cannot call it life, but after what happened, I don't know if I have a right to that. Perhaps it would have been nobler to have ended up beside you.

If I am still alive, it's only because I want to bury you with dignity, in the place where you longed to be in life – in the Land of Our Forefathers.[23] Perhaps the Lord God will allow [*us*] to attain this mercy. Every day I say [*words in Hebrew*][24] beside you, words you asked about the day before the misfortune. These words are great and eternal, the greatest heroes among our ancestors died with them on their lips. Unfortunately I don't know the prescribed prayer because I'm not a man,[25] but you'll forgive your Mummy and appreciate her good will. It's harder and harder for me to reach you without attracting the attention of the *klemp*. I make up as many excuses as I can. Quite often I carry a jug outside for rainwater, sometimes I take out or bring in empty bottles, or else I take a spade with me and bring in a little sand for the cat. Anything to be beside you at least once a day, to pray for your little soul.

13.V.1944

My darling Son! My dear little Baby! Today half a year has now passed since we lost you. Time flies quickly, but the end of the war is still a very long way off. I simply dare not believe that this damnable work of devils in human form will ever end.

I haven't written for a long time; meanwhile various things have been happening, but we're still alive for now. I write 'for now' because I don't know how much longer evil people will continue to let us live. In fact I believe firmly in predestination, and probably it will be as the Lord God determines, but little by little I'm losing hope of ever seeing the end of the war. It's all dragging along at snail's pace – after all, this is already the 5th year and we have so little time ahead of us. All that's left of us now is just a small, scanty handful of people, perhaps countable (so I imagine), none of whom knows much about the existence of any other. Exactly a month ago they took A. away.[26] The place where they'd been staying was destroyed and they were transported west. Apparently they are near Kraków, but whether this is true, God only knows, because so far nobody has shown any sign of life, but [*they're only concerned*][27] about this and that. We're all upset, because you know what he meant to everyone, but at the same time I hope nothing can happen to such a good and noble person.

We're immensely sad, dear Child. Life is so empty without you. I never stop thinking of you for a moment. You are with me in everything I do, and often in my dreams too. Only then are you alive. So my dear Little One, I prefer being asleep to being awake. In the meantime I got the *syrenka*,[28] I have moved flats, and now it's terribly difficult for me to visit you. I was there on 8 April, the day before your birthday, and I brought you some primroses, and before that some catkins, just as modest as you were in life. I hid them under a stone, so they weren't visible to the human eye, just like you. Dear Little One, spring is at its height. It's May, all the plants are in bloom, Nature has come back to life, but what about you, my darling Boy?

A year ago, one evening you went out on all fours from the veranda into the garden, you threw yourself into the freshly dug flowerbeds, into the fresh new grass and you whispered: 'Mummy, the earth smells so wonderful.' You were intoxicated by the scent of spring, but I was agonised by the fact that I couldn't hold your little hand and take you for a walk in the daytime – you, who had such a wonderful understanding of Nature and Her creations.

It made me cry so badly, my dearest Child. Can anyone understand the pain of a mother who's forced to keep her healthy, one and only, beloved child in a cage like a criminal, and not allow him to talk out loud, to laugh, or to go wherever it's natural for him to go at that age. I had to stifle all those instincts, while also watching out of the window as other children ran, jumped, played, shouted, and laughed at will in the fresh air and sunshine. Isn't it minor or even major heroism to have an understanding of the situation at his age and to endure it all so patiently? Often when the strings were stretched and we adults had no patience for him, he'd say: 'There's great injustice happening, I'm going to shout.' Those few words expressed all the pain of his little heart, the heart of a child; the poor little thing wanted to shout out loud, at least once, without restraint. He wasn't even allowed to cry. Is it a wonder then that in these conditions, with such strained nerves, he seized upon a way out of the situation, which had been in his mind for a long time as an extreme measure, and the sight of evil people reinforced the idea of it? Oh God, he so badly wanted to live, he was the most eager for life of us all, because he hadn't yet seen any of this world, except for the atrocities of this terrible war. Today, on the half-anniversary of his death, I beg the Lord God to repay the culprits for their deeds.[29]

May the blood.

[*Almost seven blank pages.*]

1.VI[.1944], Friday[30]

Dearest darling Child! There's never a moment when I'm not thinking about you, but somehow it's so difficult to write. I've spent the whole day making slippers for Daddy out of wicks, I've only just finished, and I'm going to H., perhaps I'll manage to visit you. Instead of lighting a candle for you, dear Little One, which I can't do without attracting attention, I'll make a special request to the Lord God for peace for your darling little soul, and after the war, if we're destined to live, to do something good for the poor and for the good of our country.[31]

Apparently 24 people were executed in the marketplace today, but I don't yet know what for. I instinctively stayed at home, although I should have done the shopping. I have a terrible headache.

4.VI.1944

I read a poster listing the names of the people who were shot. Some of them were killed for supporting communist bands, and 2 of them died for supporting, feeding, and protecting Jews. As well as these, 10 more were discovered at the home of a German, and apparently 30 more were found at [*illegible*] not very long ago.

H. says that Rome has been taken.[32] The rumour turns out to be true, but I can't work out what it signifies, apart from prestige for the Allies, when they're only advancing at a rate of centimetres.

This morning an enemy plane flew over (Bolshevik?) and Flak/anti-aircraft defence was fired at it. I was just laundering underwear at H.'s and didn't get at all upset, even though the guns made a lot of noise. I think the air raids make a different impression in the daytime than at night, above all [*one that is*] not as threatening.

There has been peace on the eastern front for several weeks, as if it's 'shielding' itself, as H. would put it. The Bolsheviks are somewhere outside Stanisławów, outside Kołomyja they're fighting the Hungarians, and incredible things are being said about Tarnopol. Apparently an epidemic has broken out there, something like plague, and both the Germans and the Bolsheviks have left the city. God alone knows the truth. Some people are saying that the Bolsheviks are already exhausted and won't go any further, while others claim that they're preparing for a massive summer offensive, which is meant to happen on the 15th of this month.

5.VI.1944[33]

I brought Miedzińska 2 pieces of soap in return for the victuals she has given me to date. I have no idea how to battle my way out of this situation. It's hard to refuse, because for me these things come in very handy, but she says she doesn't want the money back – she claims the costs are minimal because [*the items are issued as rations*][34] whereas for me these purchases would cost tens of złotys on the black market.

This afternoon Górska[35] was here. She told me that apparently the Allies have landed massive forces on the territories of France. It may be that the second front has already started.

This evening some German planes flew over, and cast light signals. They were lit up by searchlights. Miedzińska apparently spent the whole time sitting in the cellar in terror, besides which her door had slammed shut and she had to wake the landlord in the night to break it open.

6.VI[.1944]

I've received some more delicious buttermilk and tobacco from M.[36] H. brought a pig's foot from Górska. It already had a strong smell, but I scalded and rinsed it, so maybe it'll be of some use. But if I poison my stomach, it won't.[37]

<u>Victoria Wolf</u>[38] 'A Girl Starts Life'

An unknown author, one of many, perhaps seasonal, but her books are quite likeable, above all still written in a period understandable to me (i.e. circa 1938). Since that time so many incomprehensible things have happened, often so fantastically vile that they defy description. I wonder what the post-war generation will be like. Perhaps they'll be wild and insane, because they see all these crimes going unpunished.

I'm going to quote a sentence that has absolutely nothing to do with what's written above, purely because it suits me and I don't want to forget it.

'There is no such thing as getting over something, there is only the soothing balsam of time, which gently shifts the pain from the immediate moment into the realm of everlasting remembrance. <u>Pain flees from the din of daily life into the quietest corner of the soul. There the dead live on eternally, bathed in the merciful light of remembrance,</u>[39] which of its own accord sacrifices gloom to beauty.'

7.VI.1944

A second front really has begun on the coast of France, in the area around Cherbourg and Le Havre, where there's violent fighting in progress. I had imagined that not a single American or Englishman would get across those enormous barriers and fortifications, and yet things aren't quite so bad. Of course, masses of people are being killed fighting on terrain that's unfamiliar to them, yet they've already managed to establish so-called bridgeheads, where they're holding on perfectly tight.

In Italy the fighting is happening to the east and west of Rome, where, according to a German newspaper, the allies have gained a deep inroad. As for Rome, the Germans are pleased to be rid of the burden of feeding a city of over a million, an obligation that will now fall on the Allies!!! Rome has in any case been vacated on the Führer's orders, to preserve valuable cultural relics from being destroyed by the barbarians' bombs and the Anglo-American murderers.[40] It's a pity, my Child, you didn't live to see these times, in any case I never know what each day might bring, but [we are] getting nearer to the end.

Today it was 'Corpus Christi'.[41] To mark this momentous day, 10 people were executed in the small marketplace.

A young couple has now moved in downstairs. Please God, may it somehow turn out happily.

8.VI.1944, Friday[42]

My precious little Kitten!

   Instead of lighting candles I'm praying to the Lord God for your poor innocent little soul, for Him to receive it in His mercy and … no, I don't want recompense, I'm not demanding it any more, because He won't compensate me for your loss anyway, my dear Son. Shalom to your little soul, dear Child!

O hätt' mein Leib…
   Von Ursula Rohde[43]

O hätt' mein Leib dich nimmer hergegeben,
O hätt' mein Blut dich niemals lassen los –
Gar innig bargst du dich in meinem Leben,
Heimat und sel'ge Ruh war dir mein Schoss.

O hätt' ich nie von jenem Glück geschmecket,
Das mir dein jauchzend Sein so reich beschert.
Ein schneeweiss Tuch ward über dich gedecket –
Und ist kein Gott, der allem Schmerze wehrt.

Die Welt ist tot, daraus dein Lachen schwand,
Nur noch mein Blut trägt dich lebendig fort.
Von allen Freuden bin ich stumm verbannt
Und alle Blumen sind mir leis verdorrt.

   A poem written by a German woman, I shouldn't really put it here, but it appealed to me so much that I couldn't resist it. And I feel the same way, I imagine this view is shared by all the mothers on earth who have suffered losses during this war, whatever their nationality and origin.

9.VI.1944[44]

On Saturday evening H.'s brother arrived. Of course he came to see me and told me that the family has given up on leaving for the west, but they have moved to the city centre in Rudki, out of fear that on the outskirts they could be murdered by the Ukrainians. There are still free trains running from Lwów to evacuate people to the West.

10.VI.1944, Sunday[45]

I went to a Corpus Christi procession. The mass went on for a long time. In the afternoon Mrs R. and Z. visited me. They brought juice, biscuits, and red poppies. I was very pleased, because at least Miki had some variety. It's terrible to be trapped inside for months on end, waiting for the unknown – at least an ordinary prisoner knows when his sentence is going to end.

13.VI[.1944], Wednesday[46]

Seven months have passed, dear little Son, and life is awful for us without you. I can't write as much any more, because I'd keep repeating the same things over and over. We're always thinking about you and living on our memories. Time is passing quickly, and yet this endless war keeps dragging along so slowly. We don't know if we're going to survive it. It is terribly hard to keep going, and the enemy still has a lot of time to act. Things aren't bad on the fronts, but they're moving too slowly for our needs. How lovely it would be if peace finally came! But it seems few people want it. Perhaps if there isn't a sword constantly hanging over a person's head, day and night, he can finally organise life quite comfortably.

14.VI[.1944]

I don't like Thursdays[47] on principle. I often feel sure something unpleasant is going to happen. So this morning I went into town. It was raining. From the corner of Borysławska Street a young Gestapo man came driving along, with a dog beside him. As soon as he saw me he steered the car closer to the pavement, accelerated, and raced past me at speed, laughing insolently. He splashed mud all over me – my eyes and mouth were full of it, not to mention my clothes which were completely stained. I cried, out of sheer powerless rage and resentment, because he'd plainly done it deliberately. I had to go home and change entirely.

How do we define Western culture as represented by a young person?

If this person encounters a woman in bad weather and plays the sort of trick on her described above, without any consideration for the difficult conditions of war time, when every little thing is so hard, then we have one answer among very many that characterise the Western culture of the defenders of Europe.[48]

16[.VI.1944], Friday

Another execution in the small marketplace. I don't know any more specific

51

details. It has the same effect on the public as eating a slice of bread and butter seasoned with something spicy. Utter swine.

In the afternoon Mrs R. took away some of the things she wants to transport to the west for protection from the Bolsheviks.

Good night, dear Child, sleep in peace, soon I will say a prayer for your beloved innocent little soul, and instead of candles I will bring you a few little flowers, as soon as I am able. I dreamt about you for the second night in a row.

23.VI[.1944], Friday[49]

Dear Child, my one and only Son!

All week I haven't got around to writing anything. A lot is happening in the world, but there's no very precise information, besides which it is biased. In general the Allies are making progress. In Italy it's going extremely well. ^Perugia – Grosetto^[50] on the second front, meaning that in France it's a little harder. Lately they've cut off the Cotintin[51] peninsula and apparently they've encircled the Germans there in a fortress and in the port of Cherbourg. I wonder how it will end. Meanwhile in Finland the Bolsheviks are scooping up city after city, in short, everyone is taking care of their own interests.

Great dismay in England. The Germans have invented a new weapon[52] which they call 'phantom planes' steered without pilots, but from a distance. Apparently they are rocket bombs of colossal explosive force. They've been bombarding London and southern England with them for several days. Dreadful havoc. So far they haven't been able to invent a so-called antidote. The German soldiers call these rockets 'dogs of hell' (*Höllenhünde*).

Lately everyone aged from 14 to 35 has been registered. They're taking Poles for war work, but not as they thought into the army with guns in their hands. Immediately after forced recruitment they're being transported, apparently for several months, though the exact length of time has not been not determined.

I went to my boss P.'s place to extend my *Ausweis*.[53] He seems to be an extremely decent person. He told me to come on the 28th and to bring a photograph with me.

This afternoon I baked a tart for Daddy for his 40th birthday. Dear Son, darling Child, what an important anniversary, but you won't be there. It'll be very sad for us. We think of you all the time, Shalom dear Little One, you live among us.

7.VII.1944, Friday

I've taken 10 days leave, thanks to which I can dispose of my time freely and don't have to go out to the 'office' for several hours as usual, which takes up a vast amount of my time, spending a lot of time with strangers is not always a pleasure. It's a pity I can't spend more of my time like this. I spent all week making a sweater in a great hurry. The front is already finished, and I've started on the back. I hope the boss will like it.

For a week [*there have been*] 1–2 air-raid alerts every night, and in the daytime too. People have got used to it by now, so it doesn't make an impression. They've stopped hiding and just go on sleeping in peace. Most of the alerts are false alarms, and the funniest thing is that when the planes really do drop bombs, there's no warning at all.

H.'s brother arrived and of course he came to see me. A gypsy was under [*illegible*]. On Sunday we went to look at the damage at the station and Polmin,[54] but only from afar, because the Germans weren't letting anyone in.

On Borysławska Street 3 men were caught who belong to a secret Polish organisation. There are various rumours on this topic; above all they reveal the deep hatred of the Ukrainians for the Poles and vice versa. Some are claiming that this area will cease to be part of Poland,[55] while others are saying that Ukraine will be on the moon. It seems to me that 'where two sides fight each other, a third party gains'.[56]

Young Miedzińska has come back from Kraków. She sold M[iki's]'s watch chain, which meant I've been able to pay off some debts, and also for a while there'll be something to live on. Money flows like water, one would wish to save it, but on the other hand daily life is so hard that it's a pity to deny oneself ½ l[*itre*] of strawberries or other fruits or fat and meat; these things are an immense luxury today, and represent a fairly serious part of our budget. The Soviets are moving at a truly American rate (an ill-timed phrase, since the Americans are moving slowly), one should instead be saying at a Soviet rate. They are already somewhere outside Wilno, so we'll see what happens next. In Finland too almost all of Karelia has been taken. In Italy the G.[57] are retreating to the north, in Normandy there's heavy fighting. In Brittany the Allies keep dropping landing forces and saboteurs. It looks as if the greater part of the French population is supporting them.

My little darling, I'm trying to write a bit about everything, I have plenty of goodwill, but no talent for writing and in any case my sense of observation is not as fresh as yours was. My dearest Son, I bought you some

flowers, daisies, and I'm sending them via H. I'll try to be with you.[58]
In the morning there was a round-up in the town, it's lucky I'd left earlier,
after I got home there was an air-raid alert, and now there are some
Germans downstairs getting milk and making a terrible noise, so I can't go
down. Sleep in peace dear little Son, your Mummy is thinking of you.

[*No date,*] Sunday

I left the house, because the landlady wanted me to fetch horses to pull
carts for her from the office. While at H.'s I cut Mruczuś's[59] hair in a manly
style. He was very pleased.

[*No date,*] Monday, 6 a.m.[60]

I didn't write on Friday. All sorts of impressions, but I'm not capable of
putting them into words. The B. are getting close to Lwów, apparently
they've surrounded it and are advancing towards Przemyśl and Jarosław.
We don't know anything for certain, because for several days the papers
haven't been arriving, and yesterday they [*opened the light?*] and there's
no radio. The neighbour who listens didn't tell us anything, because he
was afraid. Throughout there have been air-raid alerts day and night, and
planes have been flying over, but without dropping any bombs, apparently
to avoid destroying the cities. The B. are expected here any day now. The
Miedzińskas have already gone, and so have all the Volksdeutsch. Their
Leutnant[61] urged me to leave without fail, and when I said that I have no
opportunity or money, he replied that the Bolsheviks will shoot me and all
young women in general. Such [*illegible*] and hypocrisy. May he drive at
breakneck speed, they've already drunk enough of our blood. On the other
hand, God grant the Miedzińskas great good fortune and happiness for
their good deeds. They have supplied me with a few provisions, and not the
worst either. It's impossible to get any bread at all now, not even for 100
złotys, and sugar apparently costs 200 złotys.

Last night I slept in my clothes, because people are saying that the
Ukrainians are going to attack the Poles. It was peaceful, except that all
night our 'gentlemen' complained. This has been going on for several days
now. It's simply impossible to believe that such a state of affairs has come
about. I'm all jittery, and my heart's in my mouth . . . Dearest Child, my
Golden Boy, why didn't you live through to this time? You would have
shared the satisfaction with us. I feel simply afraid to believe or to put into
writing that the moment of liberation is not far off now.

A transport of Hungarian infantry without guns came back to Borysław into the Carpathians. Maybe this is their *Baudienst?*[62] In any case,

they were glad to be going home and were smiling, by contrast with the Germans, who are stiff and solemn. Feigned concern about my fiancé in front of the landlord,[63] who's behaving humanely, except that the old woman wanted to me go to the *Ortokomendantura*[64] to collect the horses. Perhaps the tradeswoman has gone crazy. Me at the *Ortokomendantura*, that's a good one, isn't it? Even so they got them out and hid them. The usual peasant cunning. I'd like to write much much more, but the impressions are weighing me down and I can't put them into words. Perhaps I'll pray to the Lord God for your darling little soul, and thank Him for everything.

24.VII.1944, Tuesday[65]

The night passed peacefully. The army transports continue to move, but in various directions. People are saying the Germans are surrounded and the only route left to them is across the Carpathians into Hungary. They are going to Sambor and also to Borysław and along the Truskawiec road, and then coming back the opposite way. Perhaps these are different ones? I can't tell them apart. Since yesterday rumours have been going round that H., against whom a coup has lately been attempted, is no longer alive, and Hess newly arrived from England has taken control.[66] Apparently there are riots in Germany, and also in the western part of our country; as well as that, Britain and America are meant to be joining up with the Germans against Russia, and also Turkey is declaring war on it. As for the riots in Germany, it's possible, but I have doubts about the result, because things like that have already taken place several times before, but have been virtually nipped in the bud by an all-powerful clique of the usual kind. Apparently the authorities had already left, but as things have improved again, they've come back. People keep wading deeper and deeper into speculation, but God alone knows the truth. I take these pieces of gossip with extreme reservation, mostly I don't believe them.

This morning I was at the cobbler's and then at the Miedzińskas' place. They left for Kraków on Sunday, and there's already a refugee woman living in the flat, a Soviet I think. The landlord opened the wardrobe for me – I took a few books they'd set aside for me and a little jam and juice. For the time being I left the machine she asked me to keep for her, because I have no way to carry it. On the road there were a huge number of front-line troops heading for Sambor. They were very tired, some in nothing but their socks, or even barefoot. Yet they looked like an army on the retreat. Apparently they even threw their guns into ditches. And yet I can't believe that devil is really dead, because there would probably be some signs of mourning, and also of immense joy, because apparently he has a lot of opponents in the army.

In the afternoon a Soviet plane dropped leaflets in vast numbers printed in German. In the name of the 'German National Committee', formed out of front-line troops, they urged [*the Germans*] to stop fighting and to surrender to the Bolsheviks. Along the way they complained about H. and provided information about the disintegration of the German army in the east. The leaflets were transparently tendentious,[67] yet to some degree they fulfilled their task, because above all the local population read them, and they are inclined to believe everything without a second thought. Among the leaflets there was even a so-called *Ausweis* (in Russian, *Propusk*),[68] an item that can make it easier for the Germans to pass into Soviet captivity. That's a fine one, isn't it? It seems that without this sort of '*Propusk*', they wouldn't accept them at all. The landlord wanted to know their exact content, I translated 5 out of 10 [*words*] and told him that I don't understand German that well.

I don't know what it's like in the town, but on my street there is total peace and quiet. Perhaps in general the situation for the Germans has improved by now and they're not on the run any more? I can hear guns booming in the distance, but I don't know what to make of it all.

26.VII[.1944], Thursday[69]

It turns out I was right. H.[70] is alive, and it was just the British radio that issued the tendentious news. Yesterday we were told that the Bolsheviks are definitely already in Sambor, but I refused to believe it. Bits of gossip as usual. There's fierce fighting in Stanisławów, in Lwów, and in Przemyśl. Apparently the B. have crossed the San [*River*] at several points. A brighter time for us – the outcasts of society – is still far away, and only fools can be enthusiastic right away. I'm not going to do that, or I'll be all the more disappointed later on.

In town I met the cook [*illegible: at Baugen?*]. She and Peters[71] both left on Sunday without even having managed to eat dinner. [*Added at bottom of diary page:* 'It's a good thing I made the pullover in time!!!'] Apparently the Soviets, whom he employed, demolished the flat after they left, though I don't entirely believe that. Maybe they pinched some provisions. And in any case even if they did, those items didn't belong to them, but to the Jews from whose houses they were stolen.

It'll be worse if things calm down, because then they'll be left without work despite an *Ausweis* to the end of September. After the Rudnickis[72] left I lost my office too, which I'd been attending for a few hours every day.

This evening some people were rounded up on Stryjska Street to load freight cars at the railway station. I hardly leave the house, as it's safer not to show one's face. Nobody knows what sort of surprise one might run into. Apparently the Gestapo are back, and so are the Schutzpolizei.[73]

Troops have been billeted again. There's 1 soldier at H.'s, 3 at the Domejkos' place, and thank God nobody at mine. I'd be in terrible trouble. The one at H.'s looks perfectly quiet, about 35–40 years old. He gave her some Swiss cheese and a lemon, which she did not fail to share with me.

Dearest Son, dearest Son, it looks as if salvation is so near now, and yet we still need to arm ourselves with a good deal of patience. It's so strange that the closer it gets, the further away it is. We have fabulous July weather, but you, my little Child, are lying in the dark earth. Is it at least peaceful there, Son? Because here one is gradually losing the strength for anything at all. I dare not ask, my darling little angel, for you to intercede for us with the Lord God, but instead I beg you to forgive us for still being alive without you. We are just ordinary people, but those people, just like the rest of the world, are mean.

That afternoon

A while ago H. was here and claimed that the B. are already in Sambor. And indeed, we can hear the boom of artillery getting louder and louder.

That evening

The landlord claims that Sambor is in German hands again. We can still hear the boom of artillery in the distance. From the terrace I can see a strong glow, and in the direction of Truskawiecka Street I can see sparks spraying. God grant us a peaceful night.

[No date,] Friday[74]

I went to mass with H., and then to the cobbler's for the little shoes. Army transports, tanks, and artillery were driving along the road in one long chain. There's traffic in all possible directions, to and fro. They do not look exactly like an army on the retreat. They're in a good mood and seem fine. It's my impression that they're more likely to be setting about a counter-attack and these are reinforcements. This afternoon there were also vehicles and troops on the move together, but this time along our street towards Borysław. I really can't tell what it all means.

Apparently Lwów has definitely been taken, and they'll be heading towards us from Sambor and Stryj. They're also getting close to Warsaw.

The radio announced that Mikołajczyk[75] has gone to Moscow, with the aim of reaching an agreement. On and on it goes, it's enough to make your head spin. This morning I got 3 kg of bread for 45 złoty. The previous [*loaf*] was like clay and went completely mouldy. Milk is now 10 złoty and butter unobtainable.

I'm coming to visit you, dear Son, perhaps I'll be lucky. Sleep in peace, dear Child!

[*No date,*] Friday

Since the newspapers stopped, I've been losing track of time.[76] We don't know anything about the situation. We've heard various reports. Throughout the night from Monday to Tuesday the Soviets bombarded the city. The bombing started at half past 10 and ended at 4. What a terrible night, when you keep thinking your life is over, because you're about to be blown up by a bomb. I was downstairs at the landlord's, M. was upstairs. I prayed to God for mercy.

I'll finish this on Sunday, if God will let me live, so for now, my darling, sweet little soul, my dear little angel, ask Him to give us peace, just as we ask him for you.

6.VIII.1944, Sunday

Dearest Child! Darling Son!
The Lord God has listened to our pleas. This morning at about 8 o'clock the first Soviet patrols arrived in the city, and an hour later we caught sight of them on our street. It's hard to describe the feeling. We simply couldn't believe it.

Notes to the Diary of Sophie Urman

1. This must be Hela, Uncle Artur's former housekeeper (see 'Introduction to the First Edition', p. 32).

2. That is, in Drohobycz.

3. P[*ani*] (i.e. Mrs) U, probably Mrs Urbanowiczowa. See notes 32 and 53 (pp. 115 and 117) of Jerzyk's diary for more about her.

4. Pet name for Sophie's husband Izydor, referred to as 'M.' a few times.

5. This first entry is undated but was probably written on 26 December, six weeks after Jerzyk's death. The Christmas holidays begin on Christmas Eve in Poland.

6. Emphasis added, here and elsewhere. The Polish word '*syrena*' (or in the diminutive '*syrenka*') means a mermaid, and is also the name of the official symbol of Warsaw. In addition, it can mean a whistling hand grenade, a siren, or a hooter. These meanings are not suggested by the context. So it is not clear what *syrenka* refers to. Perhaps it was a code-word used locally or family slang for some kind of document?

7. Unidentified.

8. Handwriting unclear, but if 'H.', then probably Hela.

9. That is, S.

10. Unidentified.

11. This is a conscious or unconscious variant on, or vulgarisation of, two lines spoken by Mephistopheles in Goethe's *Faust I*: '[*Ich bin*] *Ein Teil von jener Kraft/ Die stets das Böse willund stets das Gute schafft.*' 'Part of a power that would/ Always do evil and always engenders good.' (Translation by W. D. Jackson.)

12. Emphasis added. Presumably 'Aryan'.

13. Dimwit. See note 27 in section 'Notes to the Diary and Diary Fragments of Jerzy Feliks Urman' (p. 115).

14. That is, on the eve of the Sabbath.

15. Crossed out in the manuscript.

16. That is, Sambor.

17. Ethnic Germans.

18. Difficult to decipher but probably Szaszka, whose name appears more clearly on the next page. Not clear who she is.

19. Perhaps Mrs Rudnicki (see note 72, p. 63).

20. Sophie's own close repetition of 'nevertheless'. She is right to disbelieve the assurance. Artur was still at the refinery (probably what she means by 'factory') and ended up being deported. See note 26, p. 60.

21. Bolsheviks, referred to a few times as 'B.'.

22. Perhaps a natural function at the spot in the backyard where Jerzyk was temporarily buried?

23. This was not to be granted (see too p. 87 and note 31 below and note 22, p. 92).

24. The Hebrew words '*Shema Yisrael*', one of the two prayers Sophie says every day. The third letter of the first word (reading from the right), namely '*Shema*', should be an '*ayin*' not a '*heh*' (see Plate 9).

25. She does not mean that this is a prayer said only by men (of which there is at least one famous, or infamous, for its proclamation: 'thank God who has not made me a woman'), but that men have been more knowledgeable about Jewish prayers, upon whom prayer and synagogue attendance is traditionally incumbent. This was true for centuries, indeed until modern times when (a) women have acquired greater religious knowledge and (b) men are less involved. At final proof stage: it strikes me that she is probably not referring to the '*Shema*' which, as per the previous note, she recited every day, but another prayer, perhaps the 'Kaddish', which is in Aramaic.

26. A. has to be her brother-in-law Artur Urman who had survived as a forced labourer in the Karpathen oil refinery (having once been chief petroleum engineer in another refinery) until, according to documentation from the International Tracing Service, he was sent on 14 April 1944, with the last transport of Jews from Drohobycz, to Płaszów concentration camp (famously associated with Oskar Schindler) which is 'near Kraków'. On 13 May, Sophie says 'exactly a month ago', which the documentation thus corroborates. Although the general movement of deportations was westwards, it appears that he was deported to Auschwitz, according to the gloss on Emil's testimony (see p. 94). This must have been in late 1944, before Płaszów was liberated. From Auschwitz, after the death marches began in January 1945, Artur ended up in Silesia, possibly en route to the Gross Rosen concentration camp, according to a Yad Vashem document signed by Izydor in 1955 (and corroborated by Irit who remembers that her mother told her what happened to Artur). Artur was shot by the Nazis in Jelenia Góra (which is near Gross Rosen), but the year given is 1944, which is a mistake, considering the date when the death marches began. In his testimony, Izydor gives the place of death as Wałbrzych which too is near Gross Rosen. On the headstone of his mother Hermina Vogel Urman's grave in Bytom, Artur's date of death is given as 6 April 1945 – see Plates 1 and 2 – by which time his family had not yet left Drohobycz. (Note the discrepancy between the Polish wording on the grave in Bytom and the Hebrew wording alongside the grave (see Plate 2 and my note, p. 124), but Izydor was always under great emotional pressure when having to deal with these tragic matters and not too much should be read into this.) Had Artur arrived in Płaszów earlier he might have had the good fortune to be on Schindler's list of prisoners sent from Płaszów to the

phoney armaments factory at Bruennlitz in Moravia in the Sudetenland – a deal negotiated by Schindler with the Germans in October 1944.

27. Handwriting unclear, but this is a likely solution.

28. See note 6.

29. In this paragraph and the previous one there are smudges, surely from her tears dropping on the pages.

30. The 1st of June 1944 was a Thursday. So this is misdated and should be 2 June. This entry and the following two are written in pencil. Later datings are affected.

31. Certainly a reference to the future Israel rather than Poland/Ukraine. The Urmans arrived in Tel Aviv in 1949, one year after the founding of the State of Israel. See also the wording on the base of the tombstone in Bytom (Plate 1 and note on p. 125).

32. Jerzyk too comments on the progress of the war in Italy (see Jerzyk's diary entry on 10.IX.1943, and note 20 in section 'Notes to the Diary and Diary Fragments of Jerzy Feliks Urman').

33. D-Day, which was 6 June 1944, see the reference to a second front in the second paragraph of this entry. The entry, like others, is misdated. It is clear what has happened: see note 30 and elsewhere.

34. Elaborating slightly the single word '*fasują*'.

35. For once a name rather than an initial.

36. Doubtless Miedzińska.

37. Here, mid-entry, Sophie returns to using a pen. The handwriting in pencil seems more agitated, but I don't know if this is a result of her mood or the different effect obtained by using a pencil. Pig: in normal circumstances this traditional, although not strictly orthoprax, Jewish family would not touch pig but *in extremis* it is not only permitted but required, if that would save life.

38. No Pole I have asked can identify Victoria Wolf and Internet searches were fruitless.

39. Underlined in red.

40. Either ironic or using the language of the Nazis as reported in the newspaper.

41. Here, she says 'today is Corpus Christi', but that was on 8 June – a Thursday in 1944 – not 7 June. So the misdating is consistent.

42. This should be 9 June, a Friday.

43. Sophie has pasted a newspaper cutting into her diary. I can find no trace of the poet. (See facsimile of the page: Plate 7.)
    Literal translation here by W. D. Jackson:

O that my body had never brought you forth!

O that my blood had never let you go!
So intimately you hid yourself in my life
Your homeland and blessed peace were my womb.

O that I'd never sampled that great joy
Which your exultant being so richly gave me.
A snow-white cloth was [*soon*] your cover –
Is there no God to drive away such pain?

The world is dead from which your laughter vanished.
Only my blood still bears you living on.
From all [*life's*] pleasures I am banished – wordless –
And all [*its*] flowers for me have withered softly.

44. This should be 10 June, a Saturday.

45. This should be 11 June, a Sunday, when you would expect the procession. In this entry, the identity of Z. is unknown.

46. The 13th was a Tuesday and was indeed the seventh anniversary of Jerzyk's death. But then there is a problem with the next entry (see note 47).

47. The 14th was a Wednesday, so Sophie must have got the date wrong, assuming it was a Thursday as per her remark. It could well be the 15th, since the dating of the next entry is at last correct: Friday, 16 June.

48. This is an extraordinary entry. The Gestapo man does not know she is Jewish. Typically, he has nothing but contempt for the Polish Christian woman she is masquerading as, and she reacts spontaneously and instinctively as her persona (or indeed anyone) would, which for once is easy to do. The irony displayed in her reflection on the incident – taking Nazi ideology at face value by describing its proponents as defenders of the West (to create a new order in Europe was one of their stated objectives) – shades into an almost naive non-ironic comment about an action that ranks low on the spectrum of crimes and misdemeanours committed by the Nazis on everyone they despised and hated.

49. Mid-entry: a double page has been torn out at the centre of the exercise book but doubtless Sophie needed the paper for something. It is not a deletion because this entry continues straight on to the next page.

50. These words have been inserted by Sophie, possibly at a later date.

51. Spelling mistake. Should be Cotentin peninsula, site of the D-Day beaches.

52. A reference to the V-1 bomber. The first one hit London on 13 June, ten days before Sophie wrote this entry. With Sophie's reference to the bombardments of London, the story of Jerzyk intersects with the story of my London cousin Mark Rothstein, who was killed by a V-2 missile on 27 March 1945 (see the appendix to this book). Mark, not related to Jerzyk, was eleven years and ten months when he died, Jerzyk eleven years and seven months.

53. 'P.' must have replaced 'Colonel V.B.' See note 5 in 'Notes to Introduction to the First Edition' (p. 35). '*Ausweis*' refers to ID card; also *Arbeitskarte*.

54. Nationalised oil refinery, supposedly the biggest in Europe.

55. An accurate claim.

56. Polish proverb.

57. Germans.

58. Jerzyk was temporarily buried in the backyard at Hela's place.

59. Presumably a little boy from the neighbourhood.

60. She uses pencil again at this point and continues with it until the end of the entry. This entry, dated only 'Monday', must be for 'Monday, 17 June', unless 'Monday' is wrong. It cannot be 'Monday, 10 July' because it begins 'I didn't write on Friday', but she did write on Friday, 7 July. See also note 65.

61. Sophie spells the word (referring to a junior lieutenant) in German.

62. Labour battalion.

63. Assuming this is a reference to her 'boyfriend' (brother-in-law Artur; see 'Introduction to the First Edition'), it is a bluff or double bluff because we already know that nearly two months earlier, on 13 May, he had been deported a month before that, so she must genuinely have been worried.

64. Office of the local commandant. Reprise of the previous day.

65. In fact a Monday.

66. A reference to the famous bomb plot of 20 July 1944, and thus 'H.' here (and in a second instance in this same entry, as well as the following entry) obviously refers to Hitler, and 'Hess' to Rudolf Hess, the Führer's deputy third in line. Elsewhere, 'H.' is sometimes short for Hela.

67. In the Polish these two words are numbered 2 and 1, correcting the order without rewriting.

68. Both words mean ID card. See note 53.

69. Wednesday.

70. Again, this is Hitler – post-bomb plot.

71. Peters may be the name of the boss for whom Sophie was knitting a sweater, earlier identified only as 'P'.

72. Artur's former employees at the refinery. See 'Introduction to the First Edition'.

73. Security police (see Jerzyk's diary).

74. Thursday.

75. Stanisław Mikołajczyk, prime minister of the Polish government in exile.

76. As we can gather from the misdatings.

Sophie Urman's 'A Wound Which Doesn't Heal'

Again, I am writing about the Second World War. I usually try to avoid this painful theme but as memories fade away with time, I would like to preserve them for my family in the United States. Thank God they didn't experience the war on their own skin. They always ask me how such impossible things could have happened.

I would like to dedicate this composition to my son, who died during the Holocaust.

Jerzyk grew up in excellent pre-war conditions. He was a lovely, well-developed, and cheerful child with big blue eyes and a brilliant intelligence. He loved me as I loved him and although he was always ready to share things with other children, he would never let them touch toys made by me. 'Don't touch it, my mummy made it for me,' was his usual warning. Later at school he was always top of the class, affectionate and helpful to his friends who admired him and regarded him as their leader. Even older boys came to him for advice on difficult matters (stamps, books, etc.).

He showed an unusually brave and noble character during the war, when he had to adapt himself to all kinds of situations in order to save his and his family's lives.

In 1941, when the Germans invaded our part of Poland they started with a so-called *Aktion*, which meant that Gestapo soldiers went from home to home looking for Jews whom they formed into groups and led to a square or a cemetery. Here they were ordered to dig graves for themselves and then were shot to death.

During the first *Aktion* my son and I were at home. My husband had been called to a patient and couldn't get back. A neighbour knocked on the door and said that the Germans were taking Jews somewhere. I went with Jerzyk to a Polish neighbour on the third floor and asked her to hide us. She put us in her bedroom beneath a lot of pillows and covers. We stayed there for about an hour in horrible fear. The child said he was choking. I had the same feeling, but I asked him to endure because our lives were in danger. The Germans with a big dog checked the entire building and when they began approaching our neighbour's apartment the woman got scared and shouted: 'Go away from here, I don't want to hide dirty Jews.' I begged her, kissed her hands, and asked her to keep my son only. He could play with her children and nobody would recognise him because he didn't look Jewish. But she kept shouting 'out, out'. I took Jerzyk by the hand and we went down the steps to our apartment on the first floor. On our way we passed the Germans who were going upstairs and in their fervour they didn't notice us. We entered our apartment, I closed the door and we sat there in darkness until early morning when my husband returned. On his way home he met people who had spent the whole night in graves among the dead bodies, waiting to be shot. Now, half crazy, they tried to return to their homes.

Aktionen took place from time to time under different pretexts. During one of them they hanged the most prominent people in the ghetto on the lamp posts of the main street and left their bodies there for a whole week. When we went to receive our weekly bread ration (300 g) we had to pass by this macabre sight because there was no other route. No wonder children who grew up in such circumstances very quickly became serious and mature. My son was very quiet, read widely, and wrote a great deal on pieces of paper which he collected together. His only friend was our cat Maciek who followed us to the ghetto and remained with us. Maciek had no food problems, the ghetto was full of rats.

There were different *Aktionen* for men, children, and old people. One morning the Germans decided to reduce the ghetto and organised a general *Aktion* for whole families. As we passed the Jewish hospital we saw all the patients, doctors, and nurses dead in the yard. It's not easy to forget such a sight. The Germans took us to an old school which served as a collection point from which Jews were sent to concentration camps. We spent a whole day there. In the evening some of us were told we could go home because we were still needed by the Germans. These included two doctors, a pharmacist, and a social worker, as well as their families. It was a trick. When we came out of the school, they told us to stand in the line destined for Bełżec. My husband and Jerzyk and I stood there for a while but took advantage of the moment when the guards changed and then ran like mad in the darkness.

I shan't describe the details of our return home. Everything had been burned down. We were homeless again. We made several other moves before it was possible to escape to Drohobycz. Here began the second part of our experiences.

We were again dependent on the mercy of good or bad people and felt like hunted dogs. We changed quarters and finally landed in half of a small house. The apartment belonged to my brother-in-law Artur's former Polish housekeeper, Hela, who agreed to take us in – in return for a heavy payment, obviously. She told all our neighbours that I was a friend who had come to stay with her. Of course nobody was told that four other people were in hiding. I had 'proper papers' and could move about more freely. My physical features also made this possible.

My new landlady was very religious and insisted that I accept and follow her way of life. I had to go to church twice daily and learned by heart Catholic prayers, the Christianised names of my parents and forefathers, as well as a lot of other things, including customs and special greetings associated with holidays. She wanted to convert me into a decent Polish girl in order to save a sinner's soul. I did everything she wanted so that I could protect and care for my son, my husband, my brother-in-law Emil, and my mother-in-law.

They could not go out. Practically speaking they did not exist. They almost could not move or speak for fear of being noticed by our neighbours. They read and listened to the radio news, which worsened every time. Jerzyk continued with his schemes and drawings and plans. He said once that he would not let the Germans take him alive because he knew the hiding places of our friends and other secrets and he thought that being a child he wouldn't be able to withstand their tortures and would have to tell them everything. Through the heavy curtain he watched Polish children playing in the yard and looked at me with his big blue eyes without saying a word, but I saw that he was suffering enormously. He did not go outside for about three or four months. I promised to take him out.

After a long cold winter, spring came and with it a tiny hope for something better. One night I opened the door to the little garden in front of our house and let Jerzy crawl into it. He bent his head to the ground and sniffed the earth like a little animal. 'Mummy, do you know how beautiful the earth smells?' The garden had jasmine and lilac bushes, then in full blossom, but I could not allow the poor child to stand or even sit up and raise his head. I couldn't reply because my heart was as if in a clamp and heavy tears ran down my cheeks. After a while we went inside and he told everyone that he was in paradise. It was his first and his last outing.

People must have noticed that something unusual was going on in our house. Maybe we brought too much food from the market or fetched too many pails of water from the well in the yard. Someone sent for the German police who came in the evening and started to hit my husband and the others bitterly. They thought I was a Pole who had hidden Jews, so I wasn't spared. They rummaged around in order to find treasures (money or jewellery) and were angry because they couldn't find anything. We were as poor as church mice by this time.

Suddenly I noticed that Jerzy was tumbling over. He was very pale and I thought it was a reaction caused by fear. We put him to bed and when I wanted to bring him a glass of water he grasped my hand and said only: 'Mummy, I took the cyanide.' Those were his last words. I thought that I was going mad, I became a wild animal. I ran into the street and instinctively ran to the special camp for Jews, where my brother-in-law Artur lived. The Germans had also left a few doctors alive who were needed to take care of the German refinery staff. They had to watch out that an epidemic did not start up in the camp. I approached the guards and shouted: 'Give me a doctor, give a doctor.' There must have been something terrible in my eyes because they let me in without checking my identity and even told me where to find a doctor.

The doctor was by chance a friend of Artur. He agreed to help and on our way home I told him the whole truth, who I was, and under what circumstances I was living. When we arrived the policemen had already left the place. They were somehow embarrassed by the unexpected situation. They had taken our clothes, food, even pillows and blankets with them, and said that they did not take us because they would return in a week and expected us to prepare 100,000 złotys for them, a huge sum of money. We approached the child, who was already unconscious. The doctor had no appropriate medication. I don't remember exactly but I think he cut the veins on both wrists in order to lessen the amount of poison flowing through his blood. I cannot explain today what he really did, but I remember that something of this kind took place.

To our great sorrow it was too late. The child could not be saved. The doctor returned to the camp. I knelt beside the bed, holding the hand of my child, perplexed at the inhuman pains and the slow pace of death of the child of my flesh and blood.[2] I don't remember any more how long I remained in this position. I held my son until his body began to grow cold and stiff, and the pulse stopped beating. It was nine o'clock in the evening.

We acted as if in a bad, macabre dream. It was after midnight when we decided to bury Jerzyk in a shed in the backyard, where no one would notice. We had no tools and dug the grave in the firm and frozen ground with kitchen knives and spoons. The moon was shining and the white snow reflected its light, therefore we could see what we were doing. After about two hours the grave was deep enough to cover his body. We wrapped Jerzyk in a sheet over his clothes and I put a little pillow under his head. We spread earth on him, this time with our hands. By the time we had finished it was almost day. I closed the door of the shed and we returned to the house. Both of us were paralysed. Later I would cry very often, but at that time I was like a stone. I couldn't speak or move and the family left me alone. I took no food for several days.

After a week the same Germans came again. This time they were accompanied by two Ukrainian agents. They asked for the money and when we said we had none they got furious and hit us again. I told them that they could do with us whatever they wanted, for life without our child had no more value.

They looked at us and it seemed that even bandits could have some human feelings. They robbed us of the rest of our poor possessions, but when I wanted to give them the golden 'Holy Virgin' pendant which I wore on a chain, one of them said: 'We are religious people and do not take holy objects. It seems as though the war will be coming to an end in the very near future and we have decided to leave you to your fate. You Jews have suffered enough.' Another miracle had happened, but a very painful one this time. Our rescue was paid for with the life of our son. But life went on and to our shame we hadn't enough strength to put an end to it in order to follow our child.

I will briefly describe what happened afterwards. Every day I went to the shed with an empty pail under the pretext of filling it with rain water, which was stored there in a big container. We had placed the container on the grave – which I checked constantly, praying that people would not discover it. After about a month Hela took us to the house of her friend Zajączkowski where I lived openly in an attic room. Unknown to the owner Izydor lived in hiding above me under the roof. My mother-in-law remained at Hela's.

After eight months of continued suffering and fear it was clear that the war was almost over. The Russians defeated the Germans and annexed our part of Poland, calling it West Ukraine. Life returned to normal, even for the Jews. We had more freedom, our food rations were larger, and everyone had work in his own profession. The first thing we did was to sell my last cardigan and my husband's cigarette lighter (things of great value at that time). With the money we bought an oblong case in which we put the body of our dear son. I would not want my worst enemy to see the body of a child buried for so many months without a coffin. Good people helped us to bury Jerzyk in the Jewish cemetery in August 1944. With the money we earned at work we ordered a simple tombstone for his grave.[3] We found his diary among the books he treasured so much.

We spent about a year in Drohobycz, then, after the war, we got permission to emigrate to Silesia. My husband, who is a gynaecologist, worked again at a hospital, and so did I – as a surgical nurse. Meanwhile I became pregnant and gave birth to a daughter. This was the immediate post-war period. There were curfews at night and it was impossible to reach a hospital because of shooting in the street. I was sitting in the living room, around ten p.m., mending my husband's socks. Suddenly I felt strong pains and understood that the time had come. Between contractions I went to the kitchen, boiled a lot of water, prepared the bed, put a blanket and some nappies on the table. Afterwards I placed myself in an appropriate position on the bed.

My husband was terribly worried, for he had no instruments of his own. We had no medication, no syringes. All we had at our disposal were boiled water, a new piece of soap, and a clean towel. I spent the night in terrible pain and asked my husband if I could scream. Until then I restrained myself because I didn't want to annoy him. He replied that of course I could yell if it would give me some relief. I screamed like mad and after superhuman efforts I gave birth to a baby girl. We embraced each other and cried with joy that we had an aim in life again.[4]

[Written about 1985; reproduced here in the original English.]

Notes

1. See 'New Introduction' (p. 19) for more details about 'German'.
2. Compare the comment about the speed of dying in Sophie's interview on p. 72. Was Izydor lying in order to make things easier for the boy?
3. One struggles to imagine the conversation they had with the mason, who was most unlikely to be a Jewish mason, but maybe there was such a survivor. Tombstone: see Plate 3 on p. 128.
4. According to Irit, they were expecting, even hoping for, a boy. Better, perhaps, that the child was a girl.

'To Smell the Jasmine':
An Interview with Sophie Urman

[*This narrative is based on an interview conducted by Elli Wohlgelernter in Tel Aviv, and published in the* Jerusalem Post *on 5 November 1993.*]

Like every parent who ever had to bury a child, Sophie Urman can't forget. Next week will be fifty years since the tragic day, and still, she says, 'I think about it every day, twice a day.' Her son, Jerzy, was one of the million-and-a-half Jewish children who died in the Holocaust, almost all of them anonymously.[1] What makes Jerzy different is the manner in which he died, at the age of eleven, and that he left behind a diary.[2]

'He was very mature for his age, and highly intelligent,' says Sophie, aged eighty-one, sitting in her immaculate north Tel Aviv apartment. 'He was always very good, very sweet, ever since he was born. He was beautiful, with big blue eyes,' she says with a sigh. 'I made toys for him, stuffed animals. He never let any of the other kids touch them, because his mummy did it – "My mummy made it, don't touch it, don't touch it." – because he loved me very much.'

'He used to collect stamps – he started collecting at six – and kids much older than him, thirteen, fourteen years old, came to him and asked about the stamps, or about school, and he always gave them advice. They respected him. He knew how to read and write when he got to school, before he was six,' says Sophie, her voice beginning to trail off into a whisper. 'I have all kinds of memories. I can't speak about all these things…'

Jerzy's diary, covering the last three months of his life, is not as famous or extensive as the child diaries of Anne Frank, or David Rubinowicz, or Moshe Flinker. But it is as insightful and sensitive as any written during that era. In one entry, Jerzy wrote:

> I don't have as well trained a memory as some people, who remember every small detail. Secondly, with the onset of yet more cruelties, not to mention the crimes and sadistic inventions committed by the German Gestapo, the smaller details, the lesser crimes, fade from memory. Any of these would provoke outrage even in a person of average education here before the war; for citizens of for example Switzerland, Sweden, or America, they would be absolutely unthinkable. Thirdly, at the moment of writing this, I'm not a professional writer. I'm not even a grown-up, only a 12-year-old[3] boy – nobody could have induced me for example 3 years ago to set down my impressions.

The course of events, however, induced me to do it – and also the fact that we are starting to forget these experiences more and more.

Jerzy wrote these precocious words while hiding in an apartment in a small eastern Galician town near Lvov, called Drohobycz, where the artist Bruno Schulz lived and died. Jerzy lived there the final eight months of his life, the last of a dozen places he and his family lived in since June 1941, when Germany invaded the Soviet Union.

At first they were in nearby Stanisławów, the hometown of Sophie and her husband, Izydor. They watched as the situation deteriorated under the Nazis: the first *Aktion*, the murder of over five hundred intellectuals and professionals on 3 August 1941; the second *Aktion*, on the eve of the festival Hoshana Rabbah, when ten thousand Jews were taken to the cemetery and shot into an open grave; and the establishment of the ghetto in the first two weeks of December.

Izydor was a gynaecologist who worked at a clinic outside the ghetto walls. This allowed him to smuggle things into the ghetto, like bread, or milk, which he told the guard at the gate he was bringing in for his cat. 'You could feed a cat,' says Sophie, 'but not a Jewish child.'

Jerzy, meanwhile, was making plans to go to Palestine, to be with his [*maternal*] grandparents, who had immigrated in 1930. In the garden of his house in the ghetto, Jerzy planted white mushrooms underground, which gave him good results, according to Sophie, and which he used to bring her to make soup. 'He made drawings and plans on how he would grow the mushrooms here, where my parents had an orchard in Petah Tikva – how you would take a special corner of the field and work it,' says Sophie. 'He thought always about Palestine, because he wanted to come here.'

On the streets of the ghetto, the family would see Jews being rounded up, and shot, or deported to Bełżec. Once, as Sophie says, when they went to receive their weekly bread rations of three hundred grams, she and Jerzy passed by members of the Judenrat hanging from a pole. The boy was growing up quickly, trying to figure out what was happening, while at the same time imagining the worst of what might happen to him. One day in 1942, Jerzy came home trembling, telling his father what he had just seen on the street: a German caught a little boy who had been smuggling food into the ghetto, and gouged out his eye with a red-hot wire. 'The eye was dangling on the wire,' Jerzy told him.

In a book published two years ago [*Wine from Two Glasses*, 1991][4] by Anthony Rudolf – the English writer and publisher and Jerzy's second cousin once removed – the author wrote: 'Without any shadow of doubt, this terrible episode in the life of an unknown child ... contributed decisively to the manner of Jerzy's own death.'

More *Aktionen* followed, and fear grew. Scared of what would happen if they were rounded up, the family agreed to survive together or die together. Izydor was able to secure some cyanide, obtainable for a hefty price on the black market. He passed it out to the family, and each one carried it on a string on their person, even sleeping with it. Just in case. 'I will never let them take me alive,' Jerzy proclaimed.

'My husband explained that it's poison that works instantly – you don't suffer too much,' says Sophie.[5] By the end of the year, Izydor arranged for the family to be smuggled out of the ghetto, one by one, and move into hiding in Drohobycz. There they hid among Gentiles, first in one place then another. The first location consisted of a small room, with one single bed, a desk, and two chairs. The family rotated sleeping accommodations: 'One night my husband slept in the bed with the boy and I on the table, the second night he slept on the table and I slept in bed with the boy. My brother-in-law brought us potatoes, which we put under the bed. The next day it was all frozen, because we had no heating. I don't know how we lived there.'

The family, including Izydor's mother and brother, finally ended up in half a house with Hela, a religious Catholic woman. Sophie, meanwhile, had obtained an Aryan ID card, and work papers saying she was a technical designer at a refinery plant in town. Around her neck she wore a gold Virgin Mary, a Santa Maria. 'I was this *goya*[6] – I went every day with Hela to church, to pray. It was a very comic feeling, because I knelt, crossed myself, and pretended to pray, but I said "*Moda Ani Lefanecha*", in Hebrew' [*blessing said on waking up*].

'No one knew about my Hebrew prayers. I also didn't go to confession, and when the priest gave out the wafer, I took it and put it in my purse. I had to behave like everyone because I was saving four people at home: my son, husband, mother-in-law, and brother-in-law.'

'You don't think about whether you're right in doing it or not. This is what it is, and that's all. You take it as it is in order to save a life. You have no time to think it over.' Still, she says, it was frightening to walk out in the street, even though it was not her home town and she was fairly anonymous. 'No one knew me, but still I was afraid when people looked at me. I didn't look Jewish especially, but I was always scared.'

Inside her house was a different fear, of being discovered any minute. 'Every day we heard about the discovery of Jews and the tortures they were exposed to afterwards,' says Sophie. 'Jerzy used to say, "Mummy, I know too much, I know where everyone is hiding, so if they will start torturing me I'm not responsible; I don't know what I will do."' To pass the time they read books, and Jerzy played chess with his uncle or father, or else wrote in his diary.

'Jerzy wrote that he would like people after the war to know what happened,' says Sophie. 'He started it probably because he had the need to write. Sometimes I would ask him, "About what are you writing?" and he'd say, "Nothing special." Only after his death did we see it, under his pillow. I found the whole thing.'[7]

Overall, Jerzy had been in hiding for a little over a year by the time he died. Staying cooped up for all that time was as hard on the family as it was on Sophie to watch them. 'Jerzy said to me, "Mummy, I want very much to go out for a little bit of fresh air." One night I opened the door to the little garden in front of our house and let Jerzy crawl into it. He bent his head to the ground and sniffed the ground like a little animal. "Mummy," he said, "do you know how beautiful the earth smells?" The garden had jasmine and lilac bushes in full blossom, but I could not allow the poor child to stand or even sit up and raise his head.' Sophie suppresses a tear as she tells the story, remembering how she cried then at the depressing sight.

On the night of 13 November 1943, in burst the Kriminal Polizei, the local militia who collaborated with the Germans.[8] 'First they started hitting my husband, then they came to me. They didn't know I was Jewish, they thought I was hiding Jews, and they started offending me, with very bad words, how I dare to hide Jews. They took all kinds of things, and they said they would come back in a week, and we should prepare 100,000 złotys. We said you can take everything, because there wasn't anything.'

Suddenly, they heard a sound and turned to the corner of the room where Jerzy had been cowering in fear. He had slumped to the ground. 'Mummy, I took the cyanide,' he said, and fell unconscious. The police looked on, shocked, and left. Sophie, half-crazed, went out looking for a doctor, who came and cut Jerzy's wrists to try and let the poison out. It was too late.

At midnight, Sophie and Izydor went out to the backyard, and by the light of the full moon dug a grave with the only tools available to them: spoons. After two hours, they put him in the makeshift grave. Nine months later, they exhumed the body and reburied it in a Jewish cemetery. 'It's a terrible feeling to put the child, such a beautiful, nice and good child, into the earth, and then after nine months to take him out – terrible, terrible.'

For Sophie, as it was for Izydor, her husband of sixty-one years who died two years ago [in 1991], the memory – and the guilt – are always present. 'My husband suffered the last years of his life. He couldn't forget, like me, but he never spoke about it. He had a bad conscience about the cyanide he gave our son. I couldn't feel guilty because I didn't give it to him,' she says, but you sense her words belie the truth.

The police came back a week later, took what they had left behind, but didn't report anyone. A month later, the four adults split up, with Sophie and her husband going into hiding nearby. They lived there until the end of the war eight months later, when the Russians recaptured that part of Poland and annexed it as West Ukraine. All the adults survived.

Shortly after the war, Sophie gave birth to a daughter. When she recalled this years later, she described how she and Izydor 'embraced each other and cried with joy that we had an aim in life again'. In 1949, she and Izydor emigrated to Israel; he resumed his practice as a gynaecologist, and Sophie taught music, which she had learnt at a music academy in Vienna where she studied as a teenager.

Always, Jerzy hovered nearby. Did he save their lives? His parents believe he did, which only added to their already unbearable burden. There is always the unanswerable question: did Jerzy judge the situation incorrectly – believing that he was about to be captured, tortured, and killed instead of merely being robbed by the police, or did his action indeed thwart their intended plans? Rudolf, in his introduction to Jerzy's diary, writes:

> But even if one makes allowances for his age and the terrible stresses and strains attendant upon being cooped up in one room for that length of time in those circumstances (his diary shows he knew about the executions, round–ups, etc., and of course he had not forgotten the ghetto episode), even if one makes those allowances and accepts the consequential possibility that he judged the situation wrongly . . . even so, the event under description suggests the likelihood that he was in command of his destiny. It suggests that this was resistance of the noblest and most tragic kind, just as the keeping of the diary must be accounted a form of non-violent resistance.

Today, Sophie is troubled when people question her after reading Rudolf's account of the tragedy. 'Whoever reads the book comes to me with a complaint: "How could you do it? Who gives a child cyanide?" How can people ask me who never were there, who didn't know the circumstances, who didn't know how we lived, what it was all about?' she says, her voice rising. 'People have no right. And it hurts me very much. One person, who went through the Holocaust – she understands it.'

'Looking back, there was no other way, because every day, every second, you expected to be taken away. You were always at attention. I don't ask why this or why that. I never ask people why, because there is always a reason why they do it like that. And someone who wasn't present at this time has no right to criticise. There is no reason at a time like this: there's only instinct.'

If there is no guilt, there is certainly much pain. 'I think of that day every day, twice daily – first thing in the morning, before my exercises, when I say "*Moda Ani*", and in the evening, when I say "*Shema Yisrael*".' [*The most important Jewish prayer: 'Listen, Israel'.*] 'A wound that doesn't heal you can't forget, it's impossible to forget. You go, you sometimes laugh, you do everyday chores, you go to offices, you speak with people ... But I can't forget.'

'Usually parents die first and then children, and here we survived the child, and we suffered very much. It's a shame that such a young child is gone, and we're living, but we hadn't the strength to take the poison. We should have done it, maybe, because he wasn't any more. I don't know. The pain was so strong, so strong I can't tell you.'

NOTES

1. According to Yad Vashem, about 600,000 names of children are now known.

2. The total number of diaries – whether published or known about and unpublished or still undiscovered – is unknown. Much rarer was suicide, indeed Jerzyk's is the only case known to Yad Vashem. Their archives contain details of two failed suicide attempts, and one of these was aged twenty. The other was fourteen, Natan Shragai Shmukler.

3. Jerzyk's own mistake. He was eleven not twelve.

4. Containing the back-story of Rudolf's relationship with Jerzyk's parents (for more about this, see pp. 17-18).

5. See note 2 in Sophie Urman's 'A Wound Which Doesn't Heal' (p. 69).

6. Yiddish word for non-Jewess. This is sometimes pejorative. Here its use is ironic.

7. The recollection seems to imply that Jerzyk had kept the diary a secret but this is inconsistent with Jerzyk's statement at the very beginning of his diary (see p. 101), where he states that his uncle has refused to help him. In her essay (p. 68), Sophie says they found his diary among his books.

8. See 'New Introduction' (p. 19) for more details about 'German'.

PART III

*The Testimony of Izydor Urman,
and the Biography of Emil Urman
with Introduction and Notes*

Introduction to the Testimony of Izydor Urman

Izydor Urman's testimony is raw. It cost him a huge effort to speak about those events, but he knew it was his responsibility. Yad Vashem, then much smaller, was the right place to deposit the family material. He could henceforth direct people like me to the research library and leave him alone, which, however, I refused to do, as explained elsewhere in this book; I had no choice in the matter, if Jerzyk's memory was to be consecrated in a book.

It is important for the historical record that the almost unbelievable story of Mrs Grabowska's survival is included in the testimony. One thing is certain: had she not been so decisive, she would have died in Bełżec, along with Izydor's father and other members of my family. Unlike Auschwitz, it was a death camp (im)pure and simple: six hundred thousand murdered, of whom about half were from Galicia, and only two survivors.

Izydor recalls that Jerzyk's last words were: 'Daddy, I took the cyanide.' Earlier in this book, you will have read that, in Sophie's recollection, his last words were 'Mummy...', a heart-rendingly potent difference. And yet, quite possibly he said 'Mummy–Daddy...' or 'Daddy–Mummy...'. There is no conflict between the two accounts, only heartbreak.

'The *Aktion* Is Over':
The Testimony of Izydor Urman

Translated by Antonia Lloyd-Jones

[*This testimony, deposited at Yad Vashem, Jerusalem,*[1] *includes the interview conducted in Polish by Dr A. Raba, on 28 September 1964.*][2]

Dr IZYDOR URMAN – doctor
Address: Tel Aviv, Shlomo Hamelech 98
Work address: Kupat-Cholim,[3] Tel Aviv

Contents

Dr IZYDOR URMAN

I was born in TŁUMACZ[5] on 25 June 1904. My father, FABIAN URMAN, was a high-school teacher. He perished at the hands of Nazi killers in STANISŁAWÓW in September 1942. My mother, HERMINA,

80

née VOGEL, survived the war and died in BYTOM in 1950.

My brother, engineer ARTUR URMAN, chief engineer at the oil refinery in DROHOBYCZ, perished during the occupation in WAŁBRZYCH, in Silesia. My other brother, Dr EMIL URMAN, associate professor in the Faculty of Law at the University of LWÓW, died in Israel in 1956, as the result of heart disease contracted in a Nazi camp.

My wife ZOFIA, née ARBEIT, at present lives with me in Israel. Our daughter IRENA (IRIT)[6] born after the war in 1945, is a student at the HEBREW UNIVERSITY OF JERUSALEM.

Our son, JERZY FELIKS URMAN, born on 9 April 1932, died a tragic death as a result of the incursion of Nazi thugs in DROHOBYCZ on 13 November 1943.

My sister, FREDERYKA URMAN, died a natural death in 1934.

I completed secondary school and then medical studies at the University of LWÓW. After receiving my medical diploma in 1928 I practised for some time at a sanatorium in STANISŁAWÓW. Then came 2 years as a specialist in VIENNA, working with Professor HALBAN.[7] On returning to Poland I practised in Stanisławów, as an expert witness, and at an advice centre, as a gynaecologist.

In September 1939 when the war broke out I was in Stanisławów. As I was immediately fully occupied with medical work, I was unable to get my family out of the city. The bridge at CHRYPIN[8] had been bombed, and everyone tried to flee in droves towards Śniatyn. Out on the road, the refugees were fired on from planes, and a large number of people were killed or injured. On 17 September the Soviets had already entered the city.

I continued my medical practice, and as a doctor, under the Soviets I was highly appreciated. When the Russo-German war broke out, first of all the Hungarians entered STANISŁAWÓW. They were only there for a short time. They ordered the Jews to put on armbands, but there was no other persecution. The inhuman suffering only began with the appearance of the Gestapo in August 1941. Having miraculously avoided death during a series of several actions aimed at exterminating the population of the ghetto in Stanisławów, my wife and I decided to escape from the ghetto and hide on the Aryan[9] side.

First, in October 1942, I sent my son, Jerzyk, to DROHOBYCZ. My wife escaped in November 1942, and I followed in December of the same year. All 3 of us hid in Drohobycz at the home of a female servant of my brother, engineer ARTUR URMAN.

In November 1943 a terrible tragedy occurred at the place where we were hiding. When some Kripo-men[10] entered our hiding place, my son JERZYK took poison and died on the spot.

My son's heroic death saved our lives.

The Kripo-men went away, leaving us in peace.

We escaped to another Polish woman's house, where we sat it out until the liberation in August 1944.

After the liberation I worked in DROHOBYCZ as a doctor. From there I left for the territory of Poland, via PRZEMYŚL, in 1945.

I spent a year and a half in BYTOM, Silesia. Then I continued to work as a doctor, in my special field, in TARNOWSKIE GÓRY. In 1947 we moved to France.[11]

We arrived in Israel in July 1949, since when I have been working at Kupat-Cholim.

Extermination *Aktionen* in STANISŁAWÓW

1   *Aktion* against 'the intelligentsia' in August 1941 in Stanisławów

On 1 August 1941 the Gestapo took power in Stanisławów. As their headquarters they chose the court building.

On 3 August 1941 a decree was issued ordering the entire intelligentsia, that is, Jewish doctors, teachers, lawyers, pharmacists, and others, to report for 'job assignment'. At the time I had the flu – and it saved my life. Because of my illness I could not report. Others, though, about 600 people in all, did dutifully report. None of them had any suspicion of the fate that lay ahead them. It was the beginning of Nazi 'power', and nobody imagined what crimes those degenerates were capable of committing.

Everyone was loaded onto trucks and driven off to the woods at CIĘŻÓW.[12] That is where they are buried. The farmers in the area were the first to bring news of this terrible crime. They told how the unfortunate victims were ordered to dig graves, then made to stand at the edge of them, and were executed.

Before this news had filtered through to the city, everyone was sure these people were still alive. To cover up the tracks of their crime and to avoid alarming their next victims, for many weeks the Germans went on accepting blankets and food items from the families of the murdered men, for their 'deported' relatives.

In this *Aktion* about 50 per cent of the doctors in Stanisławów were killed immediately. The Nazis kept the remaining doctors for the time being, to help in case of an epidemic.[13]

It was only in December of that year (1941) that we found out about the massacre at Ciężów.

After this, the number and variety of forms of persecution increased, including compulsory payments and robbery. They came to my house to take away the furniture. I mention this fact, though compared [to] what we would still have to endure, it was a minor detail.

2 So-called cemetery *Aktion* in October 1941 in Stanisławów

In October 1941 came the 'cemetery' *Aktion*.[14] Ukrainians and Germans with guns and dogs on leads went round the Jewish houses, and took everyone to the marketplace. By now we knew what those murderers were planning. Anyone capable of getting away ran off to various hiding places. I managed to get down into the cellar, while my wife and son fled to the house of our neighbour, a Pole. Terrified by their sudden appearance, he hid them in his bed.

The people gathered in the marketplace were herded to the Jewish cemetery, where they were shot dead.

My cousin,[15] who had managed to escape from this death march, later told me that on their way to being massacred some of these people threw jewellery and money into a stream, rather than have them fall into the hands of the murderers. For a long time after that, there were still Ukrainians sneaking out at night to look for valuables in the stream, lighting their way with torches. There were said to be lots of precious objects lying on the bottom. My cousin, who survived this hell, walked an extremely long way in a single night to get away from Stanisławów. He finally managed to reach the Hungarian border.

Thousands of victims met their death at the cemetery. The *Aktion* began at 4 in the morning. But only at 11 a.m., when a sufficient number of victims had been herded there, did they start to execute them with machine guns.

When dusk fell on that dreadful day, the 'omnipotent' KRUEGER[16] announced: '*Also, die Aktion ist beendet*'. ['The *Aktion* is over.']

The next day the Germans announced the setting up of the ghetto. On 15 December 1941 the Jews entered the ghetto. Thousands and thousands of Jews, citizens of Stanisławów and people from the surrounding area, were crowded in there. Suffice it to say that of about 30,000 Jews living in Stanisławów before the war, and of the countless Jews in the local area (altogether there were about 20,000 of them in ghetto), about 200 Jews were still in hiding after all the *Aktionen*.

At Passover 1942 the Nazis set fire to some of the houses in the middle of the ghetto. It took great effort to put out the fire. Then came more *Aktionen*, one after another, aimed at children, then at old people…

3   The 'New Year' *Aktion* (1942)

The biggest in terms of the level of destruction was the 'New Year' *Aktion*, carried out in September 1942.

Among the many thousands of victims, my father was killed in this *Aktion*. Oberscharfuehrer SCHOTT, who had a reputation for shooting his innocent victims in the eyes, simply tore my father from my arms. I showed him the *Arbeitskarte*,[17] but in vain – he tore it up before my eyes. As he took my father away, he sneered: 'Or maybe you want to go with us too?'

Everyone who was rounded up and taken away in that *Aktion* was deported to BEŁŻEC.

Mrs Grabowska

After the war I learnt in person from [*Mrs*] GRABOWSKA, a Jewish dentist, how she and her small daughter managed to get out of a railcar carrying Jews to BEŁŻEC.

Knowing that they were going to their death, [*Mrs*] Grabowska (who now lives in VIENNA, as the wife of a judge called BIEBERING) decided to escape from the railcar with her daughter. Unable to jump out of the doors, which were tightly locked shut, she tore up a board in the floor of the moving train. Her fellow victims thought she was sure to be killed under the wheels of the train, and refused to imitate her. But, determined to take any risk at all, she preferred to die that way than at the hands of the executioners. She wrapped herself and her child in a blanket and slipped out through the gap in the floor.

Miraculously they were not killed. [*Mrs*] Grabowska only suffered light injuries, then managed to find a place to hide, and so she and her daughter survived the war.

Meanwhile in the Stanisławów ghetto the Nazi thugs were going wild. The 2 MAUER brothers shot at children as they tried to escape in panic.

Escape from the Stanisławów ghetto to DROHOBYCZ at the end of 1942

Extermination[18] was inevitable. In autumn 1942 I started to make preparations for our escape from the Stanisławów ghetto.

My brother, engineer Artur Urman, had made it known to me that in DROHOBYCZ, where he worked as chief engineer at the oil refinery, there was an opportunity to hide on the Aryan side. His former servant, HELA (I cannot remember her surname), had declared herself willing to hide us at her flat.

This Hela was rather a strange person. Despite providing us with refuge at her flat, she never concealed her dislike of the Jews, which in her case had a religious foundation. She quite often mentioned the fact that the Jews had crucified Christ, and that now they were suffering for it. In any case she had (unjustified) hope that after the war we would adopt the Christian faith. She and my wife, who had been issued with 'Aryan' documents, often went to church together.

In autumn 1942, via the managing director of the health-insurance fund, I got in touch with my brother Artur, and in October I sent my son Jerzyk to DROHOBYCZ. Very soon after, my wife went there too, already equipped with a *Kennkarte*,[19] and in December I escaped in a car sent by Artur.

The tragic circumstances of the death of Dr Urman's son, JERZYK URMAN

We took refuge in Hela's flat: my mother, my wife, my son, and I. Only my wife ever went out, because she could show her *Kennkarte*, and her appearance did not betray her origin.

However, we failed to escape the vigilance of the women next door, who must have noticed something. MARYSIA MIELNIK and GENIA (I do not know her surname), who were acquainted with Hela, often dropped in at her flat. They probably noticed that she was hiding someone there. And in those days it was not hard to guess who was being hidden.[20]

On that unfortunate evening, 13 November 1943, some Kripo-men suddenly burst into the room where we were sitting. Now we know that it was Marysia and Genia who sent the murderers to us.

The Kripo-men spoke in Polish. They were probably Silesians. We stood there, paralysed with fear. 'You're a Jew!' screamed one of the Kripo-men. 'No, I'm not,' I replied.

He hit me behind the ear with the butt of his pistol, and I fell to the floor, pouring blood.

At that moment my son, JERZYK, who like all of us had cyanide on him, instantly put the poison in his mouth.

All we heard was: 'Daddy... I [*took*] the cyanide...', and that very moment my son fell to the ground.

Jerzyk had once been witness to a shocking incident. As he was walking down a street in the ghetto (in STANISŁAWÓW), he noticed a German, who had caught a small Jewish boy attempting to smuggle an item of food. The German gouged the child's eye out with a red-hot piece of wire. Jerzyk saw it happen...

When he came home that day, he told me he would never fall into the hands of the Germans alive.

My heroic son saved us all. The Kripo-men – and this can be regarded as a miracle – were shocked by the sight of the child's suicide, and went away. And very oddly, they didn't come back that night. My wife and I dug a grave for Jerzyk in a small stable next to the house. We dug it with our hands, spoons, and forks.

That same night Hela took us to the home of her acquaintance, [*Mrs*] ZAJĄCZKOWSKA. My mother declared that she wasn't going anywhere. She stayed at Hela's.

At [*Mrs*] Zajączkowska's my wife was given a small room in the garret. There was a drawing board, to give the impression that a technical worker was living there, which is what my wife pretended to be. Without the knowledge of the homeowner, I hid in the roof area of the garret. We sat it out for months and months, until the liberation.

A sketch of the author of the diary based on his father's memories, followed by notes by his uncle, Dr EMIL URMAN

(Jerzy Feliks / Josef Arie[21] / Urman)

It is not hard to tell from his diary what sort of a child JERZYK was. Unusually intelligent and bright, he was at the same time very emotional. He had an impeccable character. He was a very good child.

As soon as we went into hiding on the Aryan side he kept a diary. He wrote it on the pages of a school exercise book, with the idea that those who survived the war would find out about the Nazi crimes.

Despite his young age (he was not quite 12), he amazed us with his sharp judgement and appraisal of the facts, his mature character. Perhaps such a pure and beautiful person was not destined to live in this world.

'I won't go without cyanide,' he declared to me, when we decided to hide on the Aryan side. Probably one of the factors that played a major role in this was the bestial crime against a child that he had witnessed. It was a terrible shock for his immature mind.

His notes too have survived. After the war his uncle, my brother, Dr EMIL URMAN, typed them out, although he was already seriously ill by then. My brother loved Jerzyk very much, and admired his sensitivity and intelligence. Here is a note he left about my DEAR SON:

Dr EMIL URMAN: Comments on Jerzyk

He was in the twelfth year of his life when he made his notes, but in fact – dying tragically on 13 November 1943 soon after 9 in the evening – he had only just passed 11½.

The reader can judge for himself what sort of a boy he was; what he must have been to write like that. Seeking perfection, as his intellect developed, he became more confident in expressing his opinion – because of his totally good will – than any adult at all. Naturally, his intellectual impulses also came from the education he received. But he applied them with the precision of a scholar, which alongside a fertile imagination often produced quite simply prophetic conclusions in his ideas, plans, and drawings, which are impossible to include here.

I was moved by his tendency to think up salutary consequences for the nation[22] (and for mankind) despite the complications of the time, his apt moral judgement, sound evaluations, and breadth of thought. A chat with him was not just an ordinary pleasure, it was also stimulating, providing serious suggestions – it was quite simply a symposium, because of the irresistible charm of his young soul. He made concessions in small matters for the sake of higher goals, and demanded the same attitude of others. He never joked about important matters.

He left us suddenly. As ever, in a situation that he took seriously, he reasoned quickly and categorically, unaware that there are circumstances that can be dreadfully false and misleading. Whenever I think of this trusting, phenomenal child, I start to choke. Indeed, he was not suited to this vulgar, despicable world.

A few words on the spelling in his notes. When referring to people he loved or highly valued he used capital letters: Daddy, Mummy, Granny, Uncle, and of course for pronouns too: Him, Her – as if he were writing correspondence.

As a cover, he was careful to use shorthand: J = juif, sand = SANDOR WOLF, our relative in BUDAPEST, and so on.

Outline for the diary written by Jerzyk

[*The outline is not printed here. See pp. 109–12 for what we have called 'Diary Fragments' and the notes on pp. 119–21.*]

[*The outline is not printed here. See pp. 109–12 for what we have called 'Diary Fragments' and the notes on pp. 119–21.*]

* * *

NOT TRUE, PANIC SOWING BY *KLEMPS*.[23] Immediately after the war Dr Getlinger,[24] allegedly our relative, turned up in Brazil, where Borysław's SZACMAN, now a Brazilian millionaire, gave him his own separate villa to live in.

Note 1   TYPICAL TWISTING OF THE FACTS.[25] This is about an assassination carried out by the underground with success – the Poles are very proud of their historic act.

Note 2 *GREUELPROPAGANDA* of the *KLEMPS*, who were expecting a special payment for the fact that they knew about us. We were not well enough aware of these manoeuvres.[26]

* * *

My brother, Dr ARTUR URMAN, added the above comments at the end of the outline produced by Jerzyk. Artur also provided explanations for the shorthand Jerzyk used in fear of his diary falling into enemy hands.

These explanations are found in the text of the 'Outline' between obliques.

Mar. = Marysia, one of Hela's neighbours
G. = Genia, ditto
W.E. = Uncle Emil
Getl. = Dr GETLINGER
Urb. = URBANOWICZOWA, owner of the flat rented by Hela, where we were hiding
Jan. = Janek, Hela's brother

I confirm this statement, Dr I. Urman
Recorded according to statement of witness: Dr A. Raba, Tel Aviv, 28.IX.64

List of Places
Stanisławów, Drohobycz, Borysław, Rudki, Dolina, Lwów, Warsaw, Kraków, Bronica

* * *

List of People

Jews	Poles	Germans
The Tierstóws	Urbanowiczowa	Schrott
Mischel	Ciupkiewiczowa	Krueger
Dr Getlinger	Rudnicka	The Mauer brothers
	Marysia MIELNIK	

Note by Dr A. RABA

The statement was taken in extremely difficult conditions. Not because of any ill will or reluctance on the part of the witness, but because of the psychological and nervous state of a father who had lost his only son in such extremely tragic circumstances.

Dr URMAN, although clearly a man who is generally self-controlled and highly cultivated, has not yet got over the immense pain following this loss, and cannot control his weeping and despair at the memory of Jerzyk's tragic death. Despite his initial declaration that he was incapable of returning to those memories, after a long conversation he did acknowledge that submitting his son's diary as a historical document and sharing a handful of memories about him was a way of honouring the memory of the deceased, and of preserving his efforts to describe those terrible times.

By placing his son's diary at the disposal of Yad Vashem, Dr U. has carried out the wishes of his son, who at the start of his notes mentions that, if he were to survive, he would like to have them published.

Jerzyk wrote them in the short period when he was hiding in DROHOBYCZ. Unfortunately it was impossible to conceal the fact that Jews were hiding there from the inquisitive women next door, who could hear through the wall almost every murmur that came from the flat occupied by Hela, the former servant of Dr U.'s brother who had undertaken to provide them with a hiding place.

Jerzyk wrote his diary on the pages of an ordinary school exercise book. He did it systematically, almost every day, and his notes testify to his unusual intelligence for his age (11½), the sharpness of his judgements, his skills of observation, and his gravitas. On reading these notes one is often overcome by emotion. This child was maturing extremely quickly, caught in the crossfire of some terrible experiences.

These scant pages provide a clear picture of the utter hell so often endured by people in hiding on the Aryan side. Jerzyk records every suspicion on the part of the neighbours, every movement or noise they heard, and every object (such as the bowl his uncle used to wash in the kitchen) that could have led them to the idea that Jews were hiding in the flat.

This life in a state of constant nervous tension, beyond the strength of a child, and the dreadful shock of being an eye-witness to bestial cruelty committed by a German against a Jewish boy, were the reasons why, at a moment when he thought all was lost, Jerzyk took the poison.

Thinking back to the moments when he and his wife had dug a grave for their son with their own hands in the adjoining stable demanded truly extraordinary mental strength from the child's father, who to preserve the memory of Jerzyk shared them with Yad Vashem's envoy.

Life did subsequently provide Dr U. [*and his wife*] with one consolation: after the war their daughter Irit was born, now a highly gifted university student.

In Jerzyk's notes we often find mention of Uncle Emil, who survived the war, but never recovered his health. He died in Israel as a result of an illness acquired in the camp and then while living a nomadic life in the forest. Before he died he devotedly put his nephew's notes in order and typed them out. The original diary and a typed copy are now in the possession of Jerzyk's father.

Notes to the Testimony of Izydor Urman

[Some references have been glossed elsewhere in the book and are not repeated here.]

1. I refer the reader to *Wikipedia* and other easily found sources for accounts of the purpose and history of Yad Vashem since it was founded in 1953.

2. A few transcription errors have been silently corrected.

3. Kupat-Cholim refers to the Public Health Services.

4. That is, Jewish New Year.

5. See p. 21.

6. Irit now lives in Florida with her husband Allen. They have two daughters.

7. Professor Joseph Halban, husband of the great opera singer Selma Kurz and second cousin (once removed) of London publisher Peter Halban.

8. It has proved impossible to trace Chrypin.

9. The use of the word is presumably dictated by the occupying Nazi lexicon and world view.

10. See p. 19.

11. He worked as an obstetrician in Paris in the late 1940s before moving to Israel in 1949.

12. A few miles north west of Stanisławów.

13. One might have expected the 'degenerates', as Izydor calls the Nazis, to kill *all* of the doctors or, given the risk of epidemics, *none* of the doctors. Perhaps there was a mad logic in splitting the difference.

14. See p. 30.

15. Sandor Wolf – see also pp. 105 and 117 (note 63).

16. Hans Krueger was a pioneer: 'In the fall of 1941, seizing the initiative before the other Gestapo leaders, he proceeded to execute Jews in legally unclear situations, e.g., Jews or half-Jews apprehended without the obligatory arm-band. Elsewhere at that time such offences were still being penalized by fines' (see references in *Wikipedia* articles on Krueger and the Stanisławów ghetto: Robin O'Neil, 'Hans Krueger in Stanisławów, Kolomyja and District', in Jason Hallgarten (ed.), *The Rabka Four: Instruments of Genocide and Grand Larceny (Poland)*. JewishGen/Yizkor Book Project, 2011).

17. See p. 31 as well as note 53 in section 'Notes to the Diary of Sophie Urman'.

18. See note 8 in section 'Notes to the Diary and Diary Fragments of Jerzy Feliks Urman' for the boy's precocious awareness of the perilous situation the Jews were in. Some did not want to know. Some believed sanitised versions of the deportations. Perhaps Jerzyk had picked up on what the grown-ups were discussing or had been explicitly told. Certainly Izydor was decisive and clear-headed.

19. Also ID card; see p. 31 as well as note 53 in section 'Notes to the Diary of Sophie Urman'.

20. The first sentence of this paragraph possibly suggests that Izydor thought they might not be noticed. Given that five people were hiding, this is a bit surprising. See Artur's explanatory note about the Klemps and note 26.

21. Jerzyk's Hebrew names. All Jewish children have Hebrew names. Given that Jerzyk's other name is Feliks, one might have expected his second Hebrew name to be a translation of it (or vice versa), Asher. Jerzyk, like his father, was a Cohen, not all of whose members have the name. The priestly status and descent passes through the male line. His and my relative, Mike Fliderbaum, has the Hebrew name Arie, in memory of Jerzyk. See note 11, p. 24, for an account of Jerzyk's grandfather's name

22. This has to refer to Israel rather than Poland/Ukraine.

23. See entry 11.IX[.1943] in Jerzyk's diary and note 27 in section 'Notes to the Diary and Diary Fragments of Jerzy Feliks Urman'.

24. See entry 10.X[.1943] in Jerzyk's diary fragments and note 106 in section 'Notes to the Diary and Diary Fragments of Jerzy Feliks Urman'.

25. See entry 21.X[.1943] in Jerzyk's diary fragments and note 112 in section 'Notes to the Diary and Diary Fragments of Jerzy Feliks Urman'.

26. See note 108 in section 'Notes to the Diary and Diary Fragments of Jerzy Feliks Urman' and various comments, entries, and notes throughout this book.

The Biography of Emil Urman

Translated by Antonia Lloyd-Jones

[*Based on a statement by his brother, Izydor Urman. Edited in December 1964/ January 1965, Tel Aviv, by Dr A. Raba of Yad Vashem. The present text is appended to Emil's diary or journal, which is not included in this book.*]

Emil Urman was born in October 1899 in Tłumacz. His father, Fabian Urman, was a high-school (*gimnazjum*) teacher. Fabian Urman perished at the hands of Nazi thugs in Stanisławów in September 1942.

Emil's mother, Hermina, née Vogel, survived the war and died in Bytom, Poland, in 1950. One brother, Artur Urman, chief engineer at the oil refinery in Drohobycz, perished at the hands of the Nazis during a 'death march' from Auschwitz across Silesia. A second brother, Izydor Urman, a doctor, lives and works in Israel.

After finishing middle school, and then university studies, Dr Emil Urman began to practise as a lawyer in Kraków.

When the Second World War broke out in 1939 he was in Truskawiec.[1] From 1939 to 1941 he worked as an administrative clerk.

When Germany declared war on Russia,[2] he was in Truskawiec once again, on a therapeutic[3] holiday.

Shortly afterwards, he and his mother escaped in secret from Truskawiec and reached Drohobycz, where he was counting on his brother's help.

In Drohobycz he survived the period of the ghetto, persecutions, and *Aktionen*, and for some time worked for a Ukrainian lawyer (without pay of course), then for a Polish upholsterer; finally he was taken into a forced labour camp for Jews in Drohobycz, at the firm Karpathen-Oel.[4]

He escaped from the camp in September 1943. A Ukrainian undertook to guide him across the border, for a generous fee. But having ended up in a Carpathian forest, the Ukrainian robbed him, took his clothes and shoes, and left him to his fate.

Dr [Emil] Urman could not move from the spot, because a man in his underwear would surely have prompted the thought that here was a Jew who had escaped from the camp. Drohobycz was by now *Judenrein* and there was only a handful of Jews working at the camp.

After a few days of cold and hunger, Dr [Emil] Urman managed to stop a farm worker who was passing that way. He begged him to pass on to his brother, Engineer Artur Urman, a slip of paper with a desperate plea for help. The man kept his promise and delivered the message. Engineer Urman immediately sent clothes and food via this same person. Thus equipped, Dr

[Emil] Urman was able to get back to Drohobycz, where he made his way to 10 Górna Brama Street.

In this house lived Engineer Urman's former maid, who provided a hiding place in her flat for Dr Izydor Urman, his wife, his mother, and his son. There Dr Emil Urman hid too, after his unsuccessful attempt to get across the border.

He remained in this hiding place until the liberation in August 1944. After the liberation he went to Lwów. There he got an associate professorship at Lwów University's Faculty of Law. An essay of his has been found in the university library, written before the war, on Kant's philosophical theory of law.

In 1945 he was repatriated to Bytom, where the rest of the few members of his family who were still alive were living: his mother, his brother Dr Izydor Urman, and Izydor's wife.[5]

In 1950[6] he left for Israel. Exhausted by his tough wartime experiences, he never regained his strength. Heart disease progressed rapidly, nor could he find suitable work. He got a job as a weights inspector. The only bright point in the final years of his life was the work he did through the agency of Dr Mozes. It was to do with Israeli contracts in the oil industry.

He enthusiastically set about this work, which was suited to his knowledge and capabilities, but at the same time it used up the last of his enfeebled health.

Taken in 1956 to the Malben hospital,[7] he typed out his notes from the camp in Drohobycz. The notes were written in pencil, often illegible, but he wanted to leave them in a readable form as a legacy for future researchers.

He devoted the very last of his strength to this work.

Dr Emil Urman died on 11 December 1956.

* * *

Some facts about the people mentioned in Dr Emil Urman's diary:

Engineer Artur Urman: the author's brother, chief engineer at the oil refinery in Drohobycz. An outstanding professional. After the forced labour camp in Drohobycz was closed down, he was transported to Auschwitz. From there he was herded on a 'death march' across Silesia. He was murdered on the way by the Nazis.

Engineer Piotrowski from Kraków, who was also on the 'death march', survived it, and after the war described that grim march in detail: the prisoners were herded barefoot across Silesia. Engineer Urman did have a chance of survival, because the Germans wanted to exploit his superb professional knowledge. Unfortunately, on the way, Urman developed a suppurating wound on his hand, and began to have a high temperature. Sick people were killed en route. This same fate befell Engineer Urman.

After the war his brother, Dr Emil Urman, went to Silesia to find traces of his brother's grave, but his search was in vain.

Engineer Artur Urman saved his entire family (his wife and son, as well as his brother Dr Izydor Urman and his wife) by securing for them a hiding place in the flat of his former maid in Drohobycz.[8]

Dziunka and Marianek: wife and son of Engineer Artur Urman. They survived the war and now live in Paris.

Dr Izydor Urman (Izio): doctor, the author's brother, now lives in Israel, Shlomo Hamelech 98, Tel Aviv.

* * *

Comments:
Dr Emil Urman's diary starts with the date 19.VI.[19]43.
The heading is: Concentration camp, Drohobycz.
The notes that follow sometimes carry dates, but most often are not dated.

Dr Emil Urman escaped from the camp in September 1943. Thus, one should suppose that the 'diary' was written in the months from June to the end of August or the start of September 1943.[9]

The diary, donated to Yad Vashem by Dr Izydor Urman, breaks off on p. 128 of the [original] typescript.

According to Dr Izydor Urman, there was originally an ending, but it got lost. Despite searching for it, he could not find it.

The ellipses in the text of this typescript mark passages that have been omitted. These passages either concern the author's very intimate experiences (and have no essential significance for the entire text), or are repetitions of thoughts already expressed, or contain lengthy and complex historiosophical[10] debates on the topic of Poland's past history.

Why did Dr Urman write his diary in such difficult camp conditions and later rewrite them on a typewriter in the final days of his life?

We find the answer to this question on the first page of the diary. Dr Urman writes: 'There is no more prospect of surviving the war – but maybe it is worth leaving a few notes for people who are not destined for extermination, so that one day they can admit: *nostra culpa, mea culpa...*'

And thus these notes were to be a sort of examination of conscience for those who indifferently watched the crime of genocide...

They were to be a bleeding reproach, uttered by one of those doomed to extermination...

If Dr Urman <u>in 1956</u>[11] painstakingly rewrote these notes, as a warning and education for his descendants, or maybe for his contemporaries too, it means that he was – in spite of all – full of faith in the world's conscience.

* * *

Dr Urman starts his diary – by way of a guideline, contained in the first few sentences – with a conversation with a YOUNG MASTER, a young Polish member of the educated classes, on the topic of Polish society's indifference to the extermination of the Jews.

The opportunistic attitude of the Young Master, who represents the average Polish student of the period, the 'young blades' at Lwów University, is clearly depicted in the author's account.

The author has a characteristic talent for outlining in a few words a spiritual portrait and the physical features of his interlocutors. 'The Sarmatian[12] landscape of the interwar years', as the author calls it, takes on form and life in his description.

The author, a man of broad intellectual horizons and great erudition, frequented Polish intellectual circles in Lwów, and then in Kraków, and so his account takes on the features of true authenticity. Analysing the conditions that had arisen in Poland following the 'miracle on the Vistula',[13] the author reviles the lack of tolerance, and the *idée fixe* of 'Judeopolonia' as a phobia and fabrication of inadequacy.

Being fond of constructing historical reviews and making abrupt cuts in his historical research, the author starts his camp notes with a wide-ranging analysis of the errors of Polish *raison d'état* over centuries and only on p. 18 [of the original typescript] does his diary return to the present, namely to a description to the final days before the outbreak of war in September 1939 and the first few days after that. This is a very artistic description, the author is a good observer and is capable of recreating his impressions in a literary way.

There follows a description of the period from 1939 to 1941 in the Polish lands captured by the Soviets. The author provides many facts that aim to illustrate his thesis about the contradiction between theory and practice in this period.

The outbreak of the German–Russian war marks for the author a total, tragic change in his life as an intellectual and aesthete, entirely free of material cares, nourishing himself on conversations with intellectuals and people from artistic spheres.

The author describes the first pogroms against the Jews in TRUSKAWIEC, then his escape to DROHOBYCZ. Here he endures the *gehenna* of the ghetto and the *Aktionen*, and is finally imprisoned in the forced labour camp in Drohobycz.

His account of the ghetto is rich in extremely valuable details from a documentary point of view. The background is also interesting – the oil basin, its pre-war Jewish potentates, the material and moral decline of its citizens during the occupation, the passing of the commercial monopoly into the hands of the Volksdeutsch and the gypsies.

The author interweaves historiosophical considerations of the mistakes that prepared the ground for the fate of the Jews in the Nazi period with specific details, such as a curious memory of BRUNO SCHULZ, writer and artist, whom the author met in the Drohobycz ghetto, or the shocking description of the extermination of Jews at the cemetery in STANISŁAWÓW,[14] accompanied by Gestapo agents carousing over victims' graves.

In 1943 at the Drohobycz camp the author already wrote (in relation to Nazi crimes): 'In my view the Church carries immense responsibility.' And he goes on to ask: 'Where is the world's conscience? Is it in the Pope's heart?'

Just as in the notes he made – in the ghetto – the author reviled people who were like automata, people who were like monsters, who on the ruins of their own homes and on the graves of their loved ones went on eagerly trading, selling fake flour and rancid horse meat, anything to make money . . . so too in the camp he sees with painful acuity the nepotism of the brigade leaders, the toadying and mutual mistrust...

However, with this heightened critical gaze the author also perceives deeply moving details of life in the ghetto, and is capable of appreciating their sad beauty: for example, the description of the two poor, modest women who by some miracle were still able in the worst conditions to bake fresh bread each day, until finally they too made the journey to BRONICA,[15] the infamous forest where the perpetrators of genocide murdered the Jews.

Or this little image from TRUSKAWIEC: the description of a Jew studying the Talmud, impervious to the threat of events, armour-plated by his faith in the Almighty...

The manner in which the author perceives these phenomena testifies to the fact that this erudite, worldly man, who in his time did not scorn the sensual pleasures of this world, possessed, in addition to a bright mind, a sensitive soul.

Notes to the Biography of Emil Urman

1. A few miles south of Drohobycz.

2. Operation Barbarossa, 22 June 1941.

3. Truskawiec was a spa, famous for its mineral springs.

4. Oil refinery.

5. And the new baby, Irit.

6. After raising the tombstone to his mother, who died in Bytom (see p. 123).

7. A group of hospitals founded by the Joint Distribution Committee to help recent immigrants with special needs.

8. The parenthesis is not quite correct. Artur's wife and son were hidden somewhere else in Drohobycz. Marianek later moved to the U.S.A.

9. Compare the date when Jerzyk's diary begins.

10. A word coined by Gershom Scholem.

11. A few lines earlier he uses the word 'genocide', which was coined by the jurist Raphael Lemkin in 1944. Much of Emil's journal was written in 1943. About a year older than Lemkin. Emil and he may well have been student contemporaries at the University of Lwów. I wonder if they knew each other.

12. Sarmatian: Romantic idea about Poland's origins, descriptive of a cultural identity formed by the nobles in the sixteenth, seventeenth, and eighteenth centuries. Sarmatia features in the poetry of the East German Johannes Bobrowski.

13. The Battle of Warsaw, 1920, when the Poles defeated the Soviets.

14. See p. 30.

15. Details of murder sites and dates and how many Jews were murdered and where they were from can be found by trawling the killing sites catalogue on the Yad Vashem website (http://www.yadvashem.org).

PART IV

'I'm Not Even a Grown-up':
The Diary and Diary Fragments of
Jerzy Feliks Urman

'I'm Not Even a Grown-Up':
The Diary and Diary Fragments of Jerzy Feliks Urman

Translation revised by Antonia Lloyd-Jones

PINK NOTEBOOK

Drohobycz, 27.X.1943[1]

Because U. E. [*Uncle Emil*] has refused to help me, I must begin this written account of my experience of the Stanisławów hell by myself. The hell began for us on 22.VI.1941, with the outbreak of the war between Germany and the Soviet Union. In truth, [under the Soviets] we suffered many things,[2] but it was a mere drop in the ocean of unhappiness, blood, and tears[3] squeezed out by the beasts[4] of Nazi Germany. I don't have as well trained a memory as some people, who remember every small detail. Secondly, with the onset of yet more cruelties, not to mention the crimes and sadistic inventions committed by the German Gestapo, the smaller details, the lesser crimes, fade from memory. Any of these would provoke outrage even in a person of average education here before the war; for citizens of for example Switzerland, Sweden, or America, they would be absolutely unthinkable. Thirdly, at the moment of writing this, I'm not a professional writer. I'm not even a grown-up, only a 12-year-old boy[5] – nobody could have induced me for example 3 years ago to set down my impressions.[6]

The course of events, however, induced me to do it – and also the fact that we are starting to forget these experiences more and more.

So, because of the 3 circumstances mentioned above I harbour a fear that I cannot paint even a small part of the vast amount of bestiality of the Gestapo hordes. However, one can say that what all sorts of towns and cities of the so-called General Government and then the whole of Eastern Europe too were bound to endure sooner or later, Stanisławów was one of the cities which were to experience the iron hand of the Nazi executioner soonest and worst.[7] And if the Lord God in his mercy allows this awful war to end and lets us, some of the few who are still alive at the moment when I am writing this, survive, then I must, it will be my most sacred duty to publish this sparse description, oh how sparse, compared with the vast amount of injustices we have experienced.[8]

[28.X.1943]

I am starting with a description of our experiences in the first days of the Nazi–Soviet war.

In the early hours of Sunday 22.VI.1941[9] Daddy, as usual, was listening to the radio. I was still in bed, half asleep, when suddenly he said aloud to Mummy: 'You know, we've got a new war!'. I immediately woke up fully, and Mummy started asking questions: 'What war? With whom?'. Meanwhile from the radio loudspeaker there resounded: 'Last night German military units crossed the Soviet border. Everywhere they met with fierce resistance. In the process the fascists invaded the Soviet Union. Everywhere the Red Army repelled them to the west.' Meanwhile Mummy leaped out of bed and imparted this news to Frydka, who was already bustling about the flat, and didn't know anything yet.[10] They both quickly began to get ready to go and do some shopping, and to get some supplies – what if under Hitler there's nothing to eat! One needs to know that at the time, truly immediately[11] we took into account that the Soviets would have to retreat from this territory and the Nazis would come, we even took into account that there would be hunger, but nobody could have expected such dreadful mass killings passing all human concept.

German radio…[12]

[From the diary]
        execution of orders[13]

* * *

GREEN NOTEBOOK

10.IX.1943, Friday
A lively correspondence that prevailed before U. E. [Uncle Emil] left[14] ended in Hela or Dziunka[15] bringing a whole wad of letters, among them 2 from Uncle Emil: one for us and one for B. [*Grandma*],[16] a slip of paper with explanations, a postcard from Uncle Artur with a note added from Auntie Dziunka saying that the exchange of letters should be limited. She was actually right because during quite a short period over 20 letters and cards had gone in both directions. As it appears from these cards, this evening Uncle Emil is setting off on a walk.[17] We were full of the best hopes, especially because Uncle Artur's card too was in an optimistic tone, and Uncle Emil was not going alone too, but with a 'serious gentleman who was born there['].[18] Even Grandma was convinced.

[19]There was another event that gave us cause for our optimism, which presumably also tipped the balance for Uncle Emil's decision, namely the

capitulation of Italy.[20] Mummy brought back this news, she had gone to Rudnicki's[21] for a suit[22] for Uncle Emil. The newspaper briefly mentioned: 'The betrayal of Marshal Badoglio'.[23]

11.IX.1943, Saturday
Marysia[24] told Hela when she came to visit her that in Borysław[25] they caught a certain number of people who were travelling in a truck. Grandma immediately started to worry that Uncle Emil might be among them. We tried to calm her down as best we could, but like all elderly people in these circumstances she started to discern in us reasons for this event, which in her imagination grew to the extent of [Uncle] Emil being captured.[26] But we all understood that those stupid old women[27] are only trying to frighten us.[28] The paper brought news that Rome has been captured by the Germans. I don't know whether the news is true or not, but if it is, the Italians are terribly poor-quality soldiers if they can't protect Rome. On the other hand, the Allies too could have acted much faster... but either they don't want to or are not able. During supper Grandma kept saying that she has hot food to eat here, but Uncle Emil [is] in the forest – who knows if he is still alive, or if he has anything to eat, etc. Hela has been upstairs / in 'The Mountains'/[29] and she brought the message that Artur had been interrogated because of Melci's disappearance /Emil's/.[30]

12.IX.1943, Sunday
Today Mummy went with Hela to church. When she came back she started telling us that first Hela had gone to [meet Mr] Tierstów,[31] and then that in church they met Urbanowiczowa[32] who confirmed that in Borysław they took 8 Jews[33] from the 'Galicia'[34] refinery in a truck and that even her husband had difficulties in connection with this because the driver who took them away was one of his subordinates. Apparently all the Jews are already at the courthouse./[35] Hela has now come back from [Mr] Tierstów and is not saying anything. A few hours after dinner only, when we were sitting with Daddy at table, Hela came out of her room and said with a stupid smile on her face: 'There has been a message from Mr Emil that he crossed the border[36] and Mr Tierstów said it's a pity you didn't all go with him too.' After that she went out into the kitchen before we had time to question her. But after a while she could not restrain her tendency to chatter, and she came in, starting to talk with the same stupid smirk on her face. Mr Tierstów said that [Uncle] Emil was attacked, robbed, beaten, given away to the G.,[37] and it seems he is no longer alive. As the first time, so too the second time, I immediately had no doubt that she was taking us for a ride, but while up to this point I have thought she was keeping us out

of pure noblesse, her tone of voice and behaviour when giving us this sad news showed either a very limited intellect or *'Schadenfreude'*.[38]

Hitler made a speech. It was quoted in the newspaper. A person who broke so many pacts, promises, and agreements, he is now complaining about the breach of faith of his former allies. But excuse me using the word person for the concept of Hitler when he is the personification of the devil – precisely because he waged war through false promises, because he guaranteed the inviolability of women and children, the civilian population, yet at the present time the earth of Europe covers thousands of mass graves, in which are buried millions of victims of the Gestapo,[39] the institution which was created by him for terrorising the peaceful population and murdering some of its classes, especially the most valuable ones.[40] And that's why his closest and oldest allies have abandoned him so he will gradually bear the penalty for the sea of blood of his own nation and foreign nations, which he has shed.

13.IX.1943, Monday
So I was right when I said Hela was exaggerating yesterday purely from a desire to 'make herself important' or from a general female tendency to chatter,[41] or perhaps from pure stupidity. We did manage to find out that until now [*Uncle*] Emil was only robbed and he is now with the second guide.[42]

[* * *][43]

24.X.1943
Hela's brother arrived. The gas men appeared but instead of doing it for us they were doing it for Ciupkiewiczowa.[44]

25.X.1943
The gas men are working for Ciupkiewiczowa. We found out that Genia yesterday told Hela: 'It's a shame that German officers hide Jews',[45] / referring to Dr Mischel, a well-known laryngologist, who was alive, or maybe his daughter, who with the help of his patient – an officer – smuggled from Maidanek or Treblinka to Drohobycz./[46] Genia left.

26.X.1943
This poor Ciupkiewiczowa sold 1 metre of Amerikanki /good quality potatoes/.[47]

Marysia arrives with her sister's child. She told Hela that in Rudki they murdered another Polish priest and his children.

Uncle Emil's birthday.

27.X.1943
Marysia Mielnik told Hela that in Lwów while catching escaping Jews[48] they killed 2 Poles. Urbanowiczowa visited in the evening and said that in Warsaw, Cracow, and Krosno they are killing Poles and Jews,[49] and that Jews are treated well, that they are getting milk and meat,[50] and that new militia arrived from Lwów with ten Gestapo men, and because of that she is afraid of something [an *Aktion*][51] on 11.XI /Polish Independence day/.[52] In the entire Catholic milieu Urbanowiczowa was the only one trying to see the misery of Poles and Jews as a single phenomenon. Because of her attitude, she kept hope alive, a rather old-fashioned position, but coming from her, truly felt.[53] Hela on the other hand went to Marysia Mielnik and came back with the news that there will be an *Aktion* against Jews because the Gestapo has arrived.

Huczyńska /elderly neighbour, relative of Huczyński, who guided Izio out of Stanisławów/[54] made sure she got the potato peelings from us [*for the pig*].[55]

28.X.43[56]
During the afternoon Hela opened the window and went to dig potatoes. Andzis,[57] passing under the window, lifted it and broke the glass.

'Don't address me as *wy*,[58] I don't like it.'
'Don't slam the doors.'
'Don't watch me[59] eating from the pot, before the war I used to eat better.'

In the afternoon Hela brought a new pane of glass and beetroots. She started throwing beetroots. Then she went to Marysia Mielnik again and brought back a new knitted skirt. In the afternoon the gas man came and said that tomorrow they would fix the gas.

29.X.1943
The gas fitter is working for Ciupkiewiczowa again.[60]
I wanted to get washed but Hela said that the water for her hair would go cold. /Every morning Hela would wash her mane in very hot water./[61]

30.X.1943
The gas fitter only worked until noon for us.[62]
There were no newspapers in town, but it was full of Hungarians.[63] As

I was washing myself Hela got bad tempered[64] because there was no water left for her /in the yard/.[65]

31.X.1943

In the morning Hela went to church then dropped in. Afterwards she visited Marysia Mielnik and brought back a cat. The cat was sickly because somebody at Marysia's had kicked him. Hela's brother arrived and said he had wanted to telephone with news of an *Aktion* in Lwów.[66] Uncle Emil cleared his throat.[67] Afterwards Hela's brother went to the kitchen and started to talk there. Uncle Emil cleared his throat 8 times. At last the brother went away. When he was still in the kitchen I heard him say:

'I don't approve. The Poles are attempting the impossible.'[68]
'The Soviets are not so terrible.'
'Kiev is being mined.'
'In Rudki there was a newspaper.'

Hela was in 'The Mountains'.[69] She brought some money for Grandma but nothing written, and said there was a panic there. The hot water bottle burst.

1.XI.1943

All Saints Day. The cat meowed in the night.

In the morning Hela went with Mummy to church and at the door of 'The Mountains' in the presence of M/ischlonow/[70] and the dark girl with the plaits she gave H.[71] things as well as information that the camp in Lwów had been completely liquidated[72] and the same thing will happen here in a matter of days.

Mummy brought back all this information while I was still lying sleepily in bed. Hela went to confession carrying bags.

She was supposed to take things to Marysia Mielnik but Marysia was not at home and Hela had to carry the bags through the street. /Selling off things gave you the means to live, but it was risky because it drew attention to you. Marysia Mielnik was doing the selling./[73]

Then the fitter came, not Szk, but another one, who was working for us. In the meantime Hela was in 'The Mountains' despite having been told not to go there[74] /when an *Aktion* was in the air./[75] Then she remembered she was supposed to hand over the note from yesterday. Here meanwhile was a peasant woman with butter [*which she wanted*] to exchange for soap.

At first Grandma sat in the middle room /where if the fitter accidentally opened the door he would see her./[76] Only later she went into

Hela's room. We went into Hela's room. When the fitter finished, Genia came to the kitchen. She was sitting there for 2 whole hours.

2.XI.43

The fitter came. He went to the kitchen just when we were sitting in the middle room and Uncle Emil had just finished. 'Let [me?] push past.' Uncle Emil was moving about. Only after that with Mummy's help we went into Hela's room. Uncle Emil began to smoke a cigarette and of course he started coughing.

The fitter said that the job would be checked today, by Fl.[77] and some chap from the gas office. But they did not come during the morning and Hela was asking Ciupkiewiczowa when they would come and she said not until the evening. But in the evening they didn't come either. Meanwhile Hela took the cat back to Marysia Mielnik. Then she went to 'The Mountains' and brought back a card stating there were still 2 more weeks. Some policeman said to Chasia[78] [in Russian][79] when she wanted to go inside the refinery:[80] 'give [us] 100 roubles'.[81]

Because the people checking the job didn't come Hela went to Ciupkiewiczowa to ask her about it. She said they would come the next day. She also told her that at 1 o'clock they shot 12 hostages for 'banditry'.[82]

3.XI.1943

In the morning the fitter didn't come, nor did the checker.[83] Uncle Emil came into the kitchen and started talking to Grandma. When Daddy commented on this, Emil got quite angry. After dinner, when we had spread out our things [to sell], a car stopped in front of our gate and some people got out. We thought they were the men to check the gas, but it was just the fitter, who had brought the hot water bottle which had been given to him to repair.

In town there was a poster confirming the shooting of ten people. If by the 4th of the month the bandits aren't handed in they will shoot the next ten hostages to set an example. Marysia said the ten shot already were all Ukrainians. There were 2 Poles but the [Polish][84] Committee liberated them.

4.XI.1943

Again the checkers didn't come, because Fl. quarrelled with Ciupkiewiczowa. So we sat[85] in vain in Hela's cold room. In the afternoon Hela came [back from town and said:] 'The shot people are lying there like cattle.' Then, 'the bandits will sprinkle them with lime'. And Genia, when she came in [to the kitchen] to fetch some water: 'I was there but I saw nothing because I couldn't force my way through to the front rows.' 'First they brought 5 people and there was a salvo, and then 5 more.'

5.XI.1943

'Don't leave any dinner for me because I have a meeting with a lady [in town].' But later, after a longish time, Hela came back really furious because she had gone [in vain] to watch the executions and because she'd been told that today they were going to shoot a Ukrainian priest and 6 women. She hadn't even finished dinner when Marysia [said]: 'Come on now or you won't see anything. We must secure a place in the first row if we want to see anything.'

Hela stopped eating at once. She dressed hurriedly and left. She was out of the house for a long time, a few hours later she came back. She entered the room without saying hello, and said nothing. We made a point of not asking her anything. In the end she couldn't keep her mouth shut and betrayed to us that the executions were postponed until tomorrow. Genia told her they were shooting people for hiding Jews. Marysia said while collecting water: 'All those women are from Górna Brama.' /That was the name of our street./[86]

6.XI.1943

This morning the fitter came. He first went to Ciupkiewiczowa's to fix the gas and then came in to fit ours. It happened like this: Uncle Emil and I were standing over a map. Grandma was having a wash, when suddenly Daddy saw an old gentleman through the window. He thought it must be somebody from the gas so he immediately raised the alarm. Uncle Emil and Daddy and I escaped to Hela's room but Grandma was in a worse situation because she was washing and could only run to the middle room. It turned out that this old man was the one who was supposed to come with Fl. but had come without him, which pleased us a lot. He came with the fitter but they only took the meter and then went to Ciupkiewiczowa's. Then they came back to us and fitted our gas, but only because they got a bribe of 100 złoty from Mummy. At last the fitter turned the gas on and lit it. After a long chat he finally left and we were able to return. Meanwhile the moment I went into the kitchen someone knocked at the window. The 3 of us ran away immediately but Grandma stayed. Afterwards it turned out it was[87] Hela, who had gone to watch the executions while the fitter was doing his job and came back in a bad mood because once again nothing happened. She [blabbed?] in front of us that once again Marysia and Genia had frightened her before it turned out there wasn't.[88]

* * *

These fragments from 10 September to 14 October have been written out twice, sometimes 3 times. Uncle Emil has amalgamated them. One version continues to 24 October (this can also be found in Izydor's testimony) and picks up on 6 November, as below. The fragments could be inserted at the asterisks on p. 104 (see also note 43 in section 'Notes to the Diary and Diary Fragments of Jerzy Feliks Urman'), but I think it is clearer if they are printed separately. Evidently there were times when he just made notes, perhaps with a view to expanding them and times when he wrote a bit more. There's a third page with a few of these notes in yet another version. The scrappy and confused manuscript is a reflection of the situation Jerzyk found himself in. Later, Emil will find it difficult to clarify all the issues.

The fragments below, in the version that stops at 14 October, are headed 'The Owl Sits in the Hollow Tree'. It is unclear what this refers to. Perhaps it is Jerzyk's poetic title for observations made from a hiding place.

10.IX.1943
Uncle Emil went to Sandor [Wolf].[90] Capitulation of Italy.

11.IX[.1943]
Marysia tells Hela in Borysław they caught 8 Jews in a car.

12.IX[.1943], Sunday
Urbanowiczowa confirmed the above. Uncle Artur was interrogated. Hela told us about Uncle Emil.

13.IX[.1943]
However it wasn't too bad. Emil emerged alive.

14.IX[.1943]
Tie.[91] sending info about Uncle Emil. Lack of fuel.

15.IX[.1943]
Poster. Reaction of Hela.

17.IX[.1943]
Marysia sees my legs when she brings in the scales to weigh flour.[92]

20.IX[.1943]
Peasant came.

23.IX[.1943]
Uncle Artur sends a letter by Uncle Emil. Grandma in despair.

26–27.IX[.1943]
Emil[93] came.

28.IX[.1943]
Hania informs that Auntie Dziunka wants to see Mummy.[94]

30.IX[.1943] and 1.X[.1943]
[*Jewish*] New Year.

30.IX[.1943]
Marysia rushed in, in tears.[95]

1.X[1943]
All 3 departed.

2.X[.1943]
Marysia came. Hela left for Zbrożek's house. When Marysia made coffee she heard Emil cough.[96]

3.X[.1943]
Hela came back.

4.X[.1943]
Janek[, Hela's brother,] arrived. Janek heard Daddy and Uncle Emil.

5.X[.1943]
Marysia frightens Hela and asks about Uncle Emil.

6.X[.1943]
Mich.[97] has disappeared. J. gossips about it.

7.X[.1943]
Dr Getlinger has disappeared.

8.X[.1943]

Erew[98] Yom Kippur. Row. Urbanowicz wants to connect the gas. Chasia told Hela not to take the cards.

9.X[.1943]

Yom Kippur. Everyone fasted till evening. Story with Hela and candle. Mumbo jumbo.

10.X[.1943], Sunday

Hela heard from Marysia that Getlinger was caught and killed.[99] Afternoon. Genia came.

11.X[.1943]

Marysia left.

12.X[.1943]

Anniversary of first *Aktion* in Stanisławów.[100]

13.X[.1943]

Urbanowicz[*owa?*] came with gas workmen. Workmen digging [in our yard].

14.X[.1943]

Urbanowiczowa came twice. Mich.[101] was caught. Urbanowiczowa is digging for potatoes.

[*Only one version of the fragments includes the entries from here to 24 October inclusive.*]

15.X[.1943]

Row. Emil moved while Genia was fetching water. On the 8th[102] she quarrels with Hela because Chasia[103] told her not to take the ticket for the food rations. Strange advice, perhaps a warning. Chasia has figured out that we will pay anything for food. Hela behaves crazily.[104]

16.X[.1943]

Nothing important.

17.X[.1943]

Genia came in the morning and saw the bowl [*Uncle*] Emil is using in the kitchen. He started to move again. [*Illegible bit, maybe* Hela came.]

18.X[.1943]
They are going to dig right by our house. Hela went to town. We are [unprotected].

21.X[.1943]
Genia is frightening Hela with the news that they killed 5,000 Christians in Warsaw for one general[105] killed. The gas fitters start working again. Ciupkiewiczowa's gas is fitted.

23.X[.1943]
[Marian's birthday.][106] Poster again announcing that in Sambor[107] they will shoot Poles and Ukrainians for hiding Jews.[108] The gas fitters get drunk.[109]

[The following entries are from a smaller, separate piece of note paper, scrawled in pencil. None are marked with the month or year — those have been added by Emil.]

6.[XI.1943], Saturday
'Those Ukrainian bands.' 'The old Gyp[sy] will beat me when [??] comes.'[110]

7. [XI.1943], Sunday
Sixteen women were taken to Bronica.[111] In Dolina they hanged 6 Tartars.

8.[XI.1943], Monday
Marysia and Genia engaged in blackmail[112] because they didn't have gas. Urbanowiczowa came and calmed them down. Hela is having a discussion on religious matters. 'Keep out of it mother.'[113]

9.[XI.1943], Tuesday[114]
[No entry.]

10.[XI.1943], Wednesday
What will happen tomorrow? Pussy came.[115]

11.[XI.1943], Thursday
Nothing happened. They are taking Ukrainians into the army.

12.[XI.1943], Friday
Urbanowiczowa had a dream that 'the young woman' was quarrelling with her husband about the milk.
    The stupid old women[116] are having gas installed.

Notes to the Diary and Diary Fragments
of Jerzy Feliks Urman

[I have revised, expanded or deleted many of the notes from the first edition and added new notes, some of which were prepared by A.L.-J. Any un-annotated, un-italicised words in the main text in square brackets are Emil's interpolations. – A.R.]

1. See introductions (especially pp. 26–7) for a discussion of the dating of the first two entries.

2. A note on Emil Urman's transcript, the only one of its kind, says that the manuscript was smudged at this point. He inserted the words 'under the Soviets' for clarification.

3. Probably an accidental echo of Winston Churchill's famous speech of May 1940.

4. A common image in Holocaust literature. See, for example, David Grossman's novel *See Under: Love* (1990), especially section I, 'Momik'. Momik is preoccupied with what happened 'over there'. Section II, for those who have not read this extraordinary book, is called 'Bruno', and is 'about' Bruno Schulz.

5. In fact, eleven years old. Jerzyk's own mistake, not a transcription error. See, too, the appendix to this book for a poignantly identical misdating: on the tombstone of Mark Rothstein in London.

6. The next paragraph starts on a fresh page although the previous page is only half full.

7. Jerzyk is right. See 'Introduction to the First Edition' for a discussion of Stanisławów.

8. Many diaries were kept in the ghettos, camps, villages, etc. of occupied Europe. A large number were found after the war. We will never know how many have disappeared forever. To tell the world posthumously what had happened was the passion of many people, including Jerzyk. See James Young's *Writing and Rewriting the Holocaust* (1990), which has an important section on diaries. Jerzyk's use of the word 'few' suggests a very clear and, indeed, prescient awareness that the Nazi aim was genocide. Unless the final sentence of the long paragraph of the next entry contradicts my suggestion.

9. At this point, Jerzyk has a footnote to say 'Written from here on 28.X.', suggesting it is all one composition written over two days. The text runs on with the next sentence, then a line space before 'In the early hours . . .'. Jerzyk wrote 1943 by mistake and Emil has rightly corrected it to 1941. The typed version looks as if Emil first put a '3', then a '1' on top of it.

10. At this date, they are in the flat in Passage Olympia, 16 Sobieski Street, in Stanisławów. Passage Olympia looks very much now [1990] as it must have done then. Frydka was the maid. They lived there until they had to go to the

town ghetto. But in her article [p. 65], Sophie writes that everything had been burnt down.

11. Jerzyk wrote and then deleted '*przypuszczaliśmy*', 'we supposed'.

12. The phrase 'German radio…' appears to be the beginning of a new paragraph in the entry dated 28.X.1943. He stops mid-word, and there is nothing more in this notebook.

13. 'From the diary': this is only in the transcript, added by Emil, because this is where the separate, purely diary notebook starts. Immediately after this is a phrase hanging in the air 'execution of orders', which is not in either of Jerzyk's texts. [See new introductions.]

14. In an attempt to escape to Hungary. See also notes 17, 30, and 97.

15. Wife of Artur Urman. Later she lived in Paris where I visited her around 1990. She would not give me contact details for her son Marian Urman – mentioned in Jerzyk's notes later – who was living in California.

16. Jerzyk wrote 'B.', presumably for Babcia (Grandma) as Emil has added in the transcription. Henceforth, I will not indicate similar clarifications made by Emil for several people. Jerzyk used initials doubtless to save time but more likely for security reasons. There are a handful of other helpful clarifications by Emil which I have not glossed.

17. 'Going for a walk' is Jerzyk's code for 'attempting to escape across the border with Hungary'. Jerzyk encoded various names etc. for security reasons. See note 30. The early part of the present entry is not yet clear to me.

18. 'Serious gentleman who was born there[']. Possibly Dr Mischel (see notes 46 and 97). Jerzyk forgets to close the quotation marks after the word 'there'. He then starts a new sentence with 'It might…' but crosses it out.

19. Not a new paragraph in the original but it looks as if it was written a little later than the preceding section – the handwriting is smaller.

20. On the same date as this entry Anne Frank reports the same news with the same optimism as Jerzyk. Anne Frank had been listening to the Dutch Service of the BBC. Maybe Jerzyk had been listening to the Polish Service as well as reading about the news in the paper. This is the only date common to both diaries. More on Italy in the next entry of Jerzyk's diary and also in Sophie's diary.

21. Employee of Artur, trusted friend of Hela.

22. He uses the word '*surdut*', a frock coat.

23. Head of the Italian government who announced an armistice on 8 September 1943.

24. Marysia Mielnik and Genia who lived in the rooms in the other flat in 10 Górna Brama Street are believed by the Urmans to have betrayed them to the local authorities, undoubtedly in the hope of monetary recompense.

25. Now Boryslav, a few kilometres south-west of Drohobycz.

26. Reading this kind of comment one realises yet again how precocious Jerzyk was, aged not even eleven and a half.

27. Here, 'stupid old women' refers to Marysia and Genia and suggests that the neighbours already knew about the fugitives, who knew they knew. Jerzyk uses the word '*klempy*' but in Polish, the word for stupid is '*głupy*' – '*klempy*' does not exist. However, the noun '*głąb*', pronounced '*glomp*', means an idiot or a cabbage stalk, and is the Polish Yiddish word for 'stupid', as I well remember from my own childhood. Presumably, Jerzyk is employing a variation that was in use among Jewish Poles at the time, or perhaps only in his family. And he is using it as a noun, not adjective. (I think some of the money the Urmans were paying Hela went to these women.)

28. Literally: 'let a rat loose into one's belly'.

29. 'The Mountains' was an oil refinery. The phrase has been added by Emil to explain Jerzyk's phrase, '*na górze*', which can mean upstairs, or literally: 'up the mountain'. Emil certainly realises what Jerzyk is referring to.

30. '/Emil's/' is Emil's typescript insertion, explaining that Emil is Melci in Jerzyk's code. Elsewhere, Emil is named and his disappearance is coded. See Note 17.

31. Chief chauffeur at the refinery.

32. Her husband worked under Artur. He may have owned Hela's apartment where Jerzyk and family were hiding. The other apartment or perhaps the whole house was owned by Ciupkiewiczowa. Later, Jerzyk is very complimentary about Urbanowiczowa's attitude. See entry dated 27.X.1943 and note 53.

33. Here, and elsewhere, Jerzyk uses 'J.' for Jews, as part of his code to fool an unauthorised reader.

34. See 'Introduction to the First Edition'. Not clear whether this is the same refinery as 'Mountains'. See also notes 29 and 69.

35. Emil has added 'prison'. Jerzyk put the word for a courthouse, but used the verb '*siedzieć*', literally: 'sit', but it is always used for 'being in prison' too.

36. The Polish word for 'border' is '*granica*'. Jerzyk uses '*gr*', an example doubtless of a shortening for security reasons, rather than space.

37. Gestapo? See the account of Emil's travails in 'The Biography of Emil Urman'.

38. Jerzyk's own word, its use being a telling sign of his intellectual precocity. Jerzyk spells it slightly wrong: it should not have an 's' in the middle.

39. Here, indeed, Emil has interpreted 'G.' as meaning the Gestapo.

40. Presumably the professional and intellectual groups. Jerzyk would have remembered what happened in Stanisławów in August 1941 (see 'Introduction to the First Edition') and known of other examples. Perhaps he

knew about Bruno Schulz in Drohobycz. Most likely he did not. This is a case of editor's fantasy, the unconscious desire to 'improve' the story as in a novel. Schulz may have been personally known to Jerzyk's uncle Artur and is mentioned in Emil's unpublished testimony.

41. I am not entirely clear in my mind whether or not this is merely a typical male prejudice. Either way, it is based upon close and accurate observation of Hela and the two neighbours Marysia and Genia.

42. The manuscript cuts off here after the word 'second', so Emil has added 'guide'. Emil returned two weeks later, after the intended escape, which proves how limited the options were. See other entries and note 67.

43. Here is where Jerzy's diary fragments from 10 September to 23 October – which follow the diary in this edition – would have to be inserted, in terms of chronology. The diary breaks off at the bottom of the centre page in the notebook and, judging by how thin the notebook is, some pages must have been ripped out from the middle. The rest of the diary is scribbled in much smaller writing on a few loose sheets. See 'Revised Final Section of Introduction to the First Edition'.

44. See note 32 concerning the ownership of the house. Emil has interpreted Jerzyk's shorthand at the bottom of the page, which is hard to read.

45. 'J.' used by Jerzyk as shorthand.

46. This is an interpolation by Emil.

47. 'Metre', seemingly odd, was common Polish usage at the time. Equivalent to 100 kg. 'Good quality...' is another of Emil's clarifications.

48. See Leon Wells' important book, *Death Brigade* (1978), on the Janowska camp in Lwów. His diary entry for 26 October, the day before this entry of Jerzyk's, begins: 'There is now no doubt that the entire camp is being liquidated.' The revolt and escape of the surviving Jews took place on 19 November 1943.

49. Emil has left a bit out here. The original manuscript says: 'In the newspaper it said Lwów is now called Lem[*berg*] and St.[*anisławów*] Stanislau.' The second half of the sentence is tacked on, as if Jerzyk returned to the first thought.

50. The very rumour sounds like one of the many deceptions perpetrated by Germany as a matter of high policy to lull Jews not yet deported or captured into a false sense of relative security. The exclamation or question mark immediately following is Emil's. But it is clear from Jerzyk's wording that all of this is simply what the visitor said, in its contradictory nature. Jerzyk was sussed enough to have spotted this. Maybe on this occasion Emil didn't credit Jerzyk enough, and felt the need to make a comment.

51. *Aktion* has been added by Emil to clarify.

52. Emil's insert.

53. 'In the entire … truly felt' all added by Emil. After the war, the Urmans kept in touch with Mrs Urbanowiczowa and sent her money until she died. Had I been quicker witted, I could have asked Sophie for her address and visited her in Poland.

54. This is Emil's note. Jerzyk would have said 'Daddy'. Izio is doubtless a fraternal shortening of Izydor.

55. It says 'for herself' but Emil appears to have added the implied pig.

56. There is no line space in the manuscript, but there is another date in the margin.

57. Unknown.

58. The actual remark is 'Please don't address me by the form "*wy*" [*plural "you"*] because I don't like it.' *Wy* is the Russian – or communist – formal mode of address, whereas a Pole would use *pan/pani*. In her replies, Hela uses *pani*, or impersonal forms, which would be normal for adults who aren't related. Polish was very formal in those days. After the war, the communists tried to introduce '*wy*' in Poland but, not surprisingly, it did not stick. The point is that using it has a political connotation.

59. The speaker uses '*pani*' here. A woman is speaking – the verb ending looks like the feminine. It sounds like Sophie.

60. There's a space here, perhaps implying that Jerzyk intended to add more later?

61. Added by Emil.

62. This sentence is an interpretation of J.'s shorthand. Emil has moved it to lower down

63. The word used here is 'sand' (*Sandor*), which is Jerzyk's coded shorthand for Hungarians. Sandor Wolf was 'our relative in Budapest', according to Emil's notes in Izydor's section of this book. See also note 97.

64. Literally: 'had fleas in her nose'.

65. Emil's addition.

66. No hint of this *Aktion* in Leon Wells' book. See note 48.

67. The previous reference to Emil in the actual diary was on 13 September when they learn he is safe with the guide. And in the diary fragments on the same date and on 14 September there is more information. Obviously his attempt to escape to nearby Hungary failed. See note 42.

68. Literally: 'jumping at the sun with their hoes'.

69. Added by Emil, although the handwriting is not clear. The word used *passim* for this place is Beskidy (i.e. the Beskid mountains), seemingly a code name for the refinery.

70. Emil clearly knew who was being referred to.

71. Impossible to know who the 'girl with the dark plaits' is.

72. See note 48.

73. Insertion made by Emil. The Urmans believed, with good reason, that Marysia and Genia betrayed them. It would seem that Marysia and Genia guessed what Hela was doing. I think they were in on the secret.

74. The word 'orders' has been added by Emil. It is a strong word, and an interesting one (Jerzyk wrote 'despite the fact that she was told not to'). Does it reflect Hela's lower status as Artur's former housekeeper, despite the fact that she holds the cards? On the other hand, if it became known she was hiding Jews she too could have been in big trouble, so the cards were not quite so strong. The word also suggests – though I run the risk here as elsewhere of over-interpretation – that her presence was that of a human being who was hiding them out of religious belief and not merely for the money she was paid, even though she hoped they would convert after the war. But cf. Jerzyk's view in the entry dated 12.IX.1943.

75. Emil's insertion.

76. Emil's insertion. The rest of the paragraph is extremely hard to decipher and partly crossed out, so we have to rely on Emil.

77. Identity of Fl. unknown.

78. Chasi could be a transcription error for Hela, since Jerzyk appears to know the person. But it looks very much like 'Ch.' and is not how Jerzyk forms his H. for Hela.

79. Emil has added this to clarify.

80. It just says 'Besk.' (i.e. 'The Mountains', code for the refinery).

81. The colloquial Russian word used for hundred roubles was '*sotku*', accusative form of '*sotka*'.

82. Doroszewski's Polish dictionary cites the French word *banditisme*, from which, doubtless, *bandytyzm* derives. Here, all we get is 'band' in inverted commas.

83. Here and above, he actually calls whoever is responsible for checking the job '*komisja*', literally: 'the commission'.

84. Added by Emil

85. Jerzyk often uses 'sat' in a room. It should be noted that in Polish the verb '*siedzieć*', 'to sit', is also used for imprisonment: 'to sit in jail' means to be imprisoned, so it can carry a sense of being shut up somewhere.

86. Emil's interpolation.

87. There's another word here but it is illegible.

88. It could be that he didn't finish this sentence – unclear. The last two sentences could suggest that the executions did not take place on this occasion.

* * *

89. [*See introductions for explanation about the dates.*] In some of the entries in this section there are a large number of insertions between '/ /' marks. I have edited these out to simplify the reading.

90. See note 63. Does this mean Emil attempted to go to Budapest or at least to Hungary? If so, he was already back by October 26. 'Wolf' is an addition of Emil's.

91. 'Tie.' = Tierstów the chauffeur. See note 31.

92. See note 73. It would not have been hard for them to guess the secret, even if they weren't officially in the know. See also note 24 and the diary entry dated 11.IX.1943, less than a week before Jerzyk's fragment, which this note glosses. It is impossible to establish the exact date they found out about the fugitives.

93. See note 67.

94. In one version this is on 29.IX.1943. Jerzyk first wrote H., then seems to have added '–ania' so it's probably not a mistake for Hela or Genia, but a bit odd.

95. 30.IX.1943 in one version.

96. Also, in this instance, presumably, either Marysia makes a comment, or Jerzyk is assuming she hears the cough. Did Hela swear them to secrecy, perhaps offer them some money? (See also note 27.) Hela's brother (see Jerzyk's fragment entry for 4.X[.1943]) could have been in on the betrayal too.

97. Dr Mischel.

98. '*Erew*' ('eve'), in Hebrew in the original. (The usual English transcription is '*erev*'). Jewish festivals begin the night before. See *Lvov Ghetto Diary* (1990) for Rabbi Kahane's account of Yom Kippur in 1943 while he was in hiding in the Ukrainian Archbishop's palace. In the sewers too, Yom Kippur was being observed (see Marshall's 1990 work *In the Sewers of Lvov*).

99. In fact Dr Getlinger survived in Sambor. After the war he got to Brazil and 'was given a villa to live in by the millionaire Schatzman from Borysław'. Emil says there was no panic.

100. Second anniversary and the second *Aktion*, which was on a much larger scale. See introductions.

101. See note 104.

102. A reference to the row mentioned in the entry dated 8.X.1943.

103. Chasia cannot be Hela, given the context of this reference. Could it be the first name of Ciupkiewiczowa?

104. After the first two sentences, everything appears to have been added by Emil and is nowhere to be seen in Jerzyk's text, though Jerzyk does mention the fact that Chasia told Hela not to take [*ration*] cards – see 8.X.1943 – but Emil has omitted it there.

105. It is difficult to read but could be '*za gener. kt. j. zab.*', probably '*za generała, którego zabili Juden*' meaning 'for a general whom the Jews killed'. According to the eminent Polish historian [*personal communication by e-mail*] Professor Andrzej Paczkowski, 'As far as I could verify, there was a huge round-up in Warsaw on 21 October 1943 but no public executions or reprisals. The public executions in Warsaw began on 16 October 1942, and the biggest was on 29–30 May 1943, when nearly five hundred people were shot. The one and only German general killed in Poland was Franz Kutschera on 1 February 1944, in the centre of Warsaw.' Clearly Genia's 'news' is a rumour, possibly invented or 'improved' by Genia as in Chinese whispers. See too Artur's 'Note 1' in Izydor's testimony in this book, where he talks of a 'typical twisting of the facts'.

106. Jerzyk's cousin, Auntie Dziunka's son. See note 15.

107. Sambor is about thirty miles north-west of Drohobycz. By this time the town had been declared *Judenrein* after the usual mass murders and atrocities. In 1944 Jews who had been in hiding were found and executed. The *Encyclopaedia Judaica* does not record the fate of their hosts, assuming some actually were hidden by Poles. A rare example was the family that hid Dr Getlinger and his family.

108. Jerzyk does not say how he knows about this poster. Presumably he overheard Marysia/Genia telling Hela. The reason they would have told Hela was to draw attention to the danger she was courting – and by extension or implication themselves – with the further implication that a monetary value should be placed upon this danger. It is indeed the case that anyone found harbouring a Jew would be publicly hanged. If you changed your mind about hiding someone and threw them out and they were captured, under torture they might reveal who had sheltered them. What to do? One solution was to murder them yourself. In the cemetery at Stanisławów there is a grave apart from the regular ones, close to the mass grave of the victims of *Aktionen*. Rabbi Viktor Kalesnik explained to me that it is the only one of its kind because the dead did not die in an *Aktion*. A woman and her four children were being hidden by a Pole who, one day, cognisant of the risks attendant both upon hiding them and throwing them out, murdered two of the children. Before the job could be completed the woman fled and then killed herself and the other two children. This is their grave. See too Artur's notes in Izydor's testimony in this book.

109. The final entry, 24.X.1943, has been moved by Emily to the main diary, although it is just as sketchy as the others from 10 September to here. It fits well with the diary entry dated 25.X.1943.

110. Emil has left gaps here.

111. Local forest used by the Nazis for murder, what they would have called executions. Fifteen thousand people are buried in mass graves, eleven thousand of them Jews.

112. That is, emotional blackmail.

113. Jerzyk quotes snatches of conversation without prefacing them with an indication of the speaker. In this instance, as it happens, it could be either himself or one of the neighbours talking to the older 'mother', Urbanowiczowa. One dare not read too much into his language, but the pressure of events upon his mind is clearly released as linguistic energy. The movement of sentences in, for example, the main entry dated 6.XI.1943, is very different from the two entries in the Pink Notebook, which are the beginning of a historical account, rather than diary entries (see note 1 regarding dating).

114. This is the only occasion where the transcript gives a date without an entry. Jerzyk made quick notes, intending to write more later, which he managed for some days but not for others. This scrap of paper is an example of the notes – he probably wrote people's remarks as a reminder.

115. Jerzyk loved the cat. See also 'New Introduction' on their Stanisławów ghetto cat.

116. See note 27 et al.

Plates 1–28 and Accompanying Notes

Plate 1. Photograph of the grave of Hermina Vogel Urman
Plate 2. Hebrew wording alongside photograph of grave in memorial book

The Polish wording on the headstone reads:
Hermina Urmanowa
née Vogel
born 21 7 1874 in Stanisławów
The model of a courageous woman
Adored mother
Died 18 1 1950 in Bytom
By a tragic death they preceded her:
Husband Fabian, Teacher
Born [*day illegible*] 3 1873, Perished [*day illegible*] 9 1942
Son Artur, Chemical Engineer
Born 12 3 1897, Perished 6 4 1945
Grandson Jerzy Feliks
Born 9 4 1932, Perished 13 11 1943

Immediately underneath the Polish, the Hebrew reads:
On the left : Cohanim
On the right : acronym meaning 'May the Lord revenge his blood'
On the base of the tombstone : Faithful daughter of Zion who never made it
to our country

Alongside the photograph in the memorial book, the Hebrew words, composed by Izydor Urman, read:

In eternal memory of my parents and my brothers, may their memory be
a blessing

My father: Fabian (Feivel-Shraga) Urman *hacohen*, may his memory
be a blessing, perished in the Holocaust 1942

My mother: Hermina Urman, from the Vogel family, born 1874 and died
1950

My brother: Arthur Urman – engineer born 1897, died 1945

My brother: Dr Emil Urman born 1898, died 1956 in Israel

The five Hebrew letters stand for:

'May their souls be bound up in the bond of eternal life'

Memorialised by Dr Isidore Urman, Tel Aviv

Tombstone and grave of our mother in the cemetery, Bytom, Poland

Note to Plates 1 and 2; inscriptions and texts

1. and 2. In the Polish wording (which would have been composed by Emil, who was still living in Poland – probably, until her death, with his mother – doubtless with the help of Izydor, already in Israel), there is a clear distinction between Hermina who 'died' (*'zgasła'*) of natural causes after the war and her husband, oldest son and grandson who predeceased her and 'perished' (i.e. were killed, as implied by the Polish word *'zginął'*) as victims of the Holocaust. (In their own way, Hermina and the other survivors were also victims, but they were not defeated. And nor, I believe, was Jerzyk. He was a hero in a tragedy.)

'Heh/Yud/Daled', the Hebrew acronym on the tombstone – which stands for the words '*Hashem Yikom Damo*' ('God will revenge his blood') – has been the standard phrase (hence the acronym) since the Middle Ages in response to the death of martyrs, and is based on well known verses in Deuteronomy, Job and the book of Jeremiah. Versions of the phrase are found in Jewish liturgy, for example in the prayer '*Avinu Malkenu*' and the important memorial prayer '*Av Harachamim*', written, it is said, in response to the First Crusade, and citing the relevant verses of the Torah. On the subject of *Cohanim* (priests), in Hebrew on the tombstone, see note 10, in the section 'Notes to New Introduction', about Fabian's name. See 20 for details of the movements of Izydor and Sophie and their little daughter after the war, culminating in their arrival in Israel in 1949.

The photograph of the *matseva*, the tombstone, was published in 1976 in the *Memorial Book of Tlumacz*, the home town of Fabian (see Bibliography and p. 21), and Izydor added the Hebrew note printed alongside for the book. The word above his name, '*hamnatseach*', is best interpreted as above, and is used on several pages in the *Memorial Book* by different families. Izydor uses the Hebrew word, '*nispah*' ('perish') only for Fabian; for his mother and two brothers he uses the word '*niftar*' ('died'), even though, in one of two accounts of his brother's death (see p. 60), Artur too was murdered. Also, Jerzyk is not mentioned in the Hebrew. I think Izydor recoiled from this partly because of the ferocious Hebrew acronym already included on the mainly Polish-language tombstone. See also the note below for the photo of Jerzyk's tombstone in Drohobycz. The five Hebrew letters I refer to above are always found on tombstones. I suspect that they were omitted by mistake when the tombstone was raised – in 1950; tombstones are traditionally raised not later than eleven months after the death of the person – and that Izydor rectified this by including them in the Hebrew text for the memorial book in 1976. Emil left Poland for Israel in 1950 (see p. 94), after the raising of the tombstone of Hermina. He died in Israel, according to various sources including the Hebrew text quoted, in 1956. (He was born either in 1898 or in 1899.)

The raising of such a tombstone in 1950 is of considerable interest, according to my friend, the political scientist, Michael Pinto-Duschinsky. Sourcing a contemporary study published for the American Jewish Committee, Pinto-Duschinsky explains the circumstances of various groups after the boundaries of Poland and Russia moved westwards, with the Silesian Germans being expelled to Germany's diminished territories.

Poles from the eastern territories which became part of Russia were moved to Poland's new lands in Silesia. Among them were Jewish survivors from Russia. Thus, Silesia briefly became one of Poland's areas most populated by Jews. They tended to move out of Silesia partly because of Polish anti-Semitism, partly because they did not feel comfortable in the lands where the Nazi Holocaust had been perpetrated. As the Communists took over Poland, it became harder for Jews to obtain permission to leave. In 1949, Jews were allowed to leave provided they left their belongings behind and provided they left by August 1950. (Bernard D. Weinryb's 'Polish Jews Under Soviet Rule'. In Peter Meyer (ed.), *Jews in the Soviet Satellites*, Syracuse University Press, New York, 1953, p. 310.)

This fits in exactly with the date on the tombstone: Hermina died on 18 January 1950 and Emil would have had time to raise the tombstone within the traditional period and still leave by August.

According to the historian of Polish-Jewish studies, Antony Polonsky, the way the tombstone is worded is 'somewhat surprising, but you could clearly get away with a lot, provided you wrote it in Hebrew. In Bytom there probably wasn't a censor who could read Hebrew. I am reminded of the two inscriptions in the Holocaust memorial in the Marais in Paris. The one in French is quite anodyne and that in Hebrew castigates France for betraying its Jewish citizens (personal communication)'. The phrase on Hermina's tombstone 'faithful daughter of Zion who never made it to our country' chimes with Zionist emotion in Sophie's diary (see p. 45, and also p. 30) and we should remember that Sophie's parents emigrated to Palestine in 1930, where she and her husband and son visited them later on.

Plate 3. Photograph of the tombstone of Jerzy Feliks Urman in Drohobycz

The wording is:
Jerzy Feliks Urman
born 9.IV.1932 died 13.XI.1943
Only son
Innocent victim of thugs
under the banner of Hitler

Note to Plate 3 inscription
3. The word for 'died', '*zmarł*', here in abbreviated form '*zm*', is a standard word without the connotation of perished. – see the note on the gravestone in Bytom. The hands on Jerzyk's tomb signify he is a Cohen.

All family photos are my copyright on behalf of Irit and family. Apart from the maps, some of the photographs were supplied in high-resolution JPEGs by Yad Vashem, to whom I am grateful.

Plate 1. See notes on pp. 123–4

לזכר עולם
להורי ולאחי ז"ל

אבי : פביאן (פייוול-שרגא) אורמן
הכהן ז"ל, נספה בשואה 1942
אמי : הרמינה אורמן, סבית פוגל
נולדה 1874 ונפטרה 1950
אחי : ארטור אורמן — מהנדס
נולד 1897, נפטר 1945
אחי : ד"ר אמיל אורמן
נולד 1898, נפטר 1956 בארץ

ת.נ.צ.ב.ה.

המנציח
ד"ר איזידור אורמן
תל-אביב

מצבה של אמנו
בבית הקברות ביטום
פולין

המצבה על קברו של יז׳ פליקס אורמן. א־157/2287

Plates 2 and 3. See notes on pp. 123–5

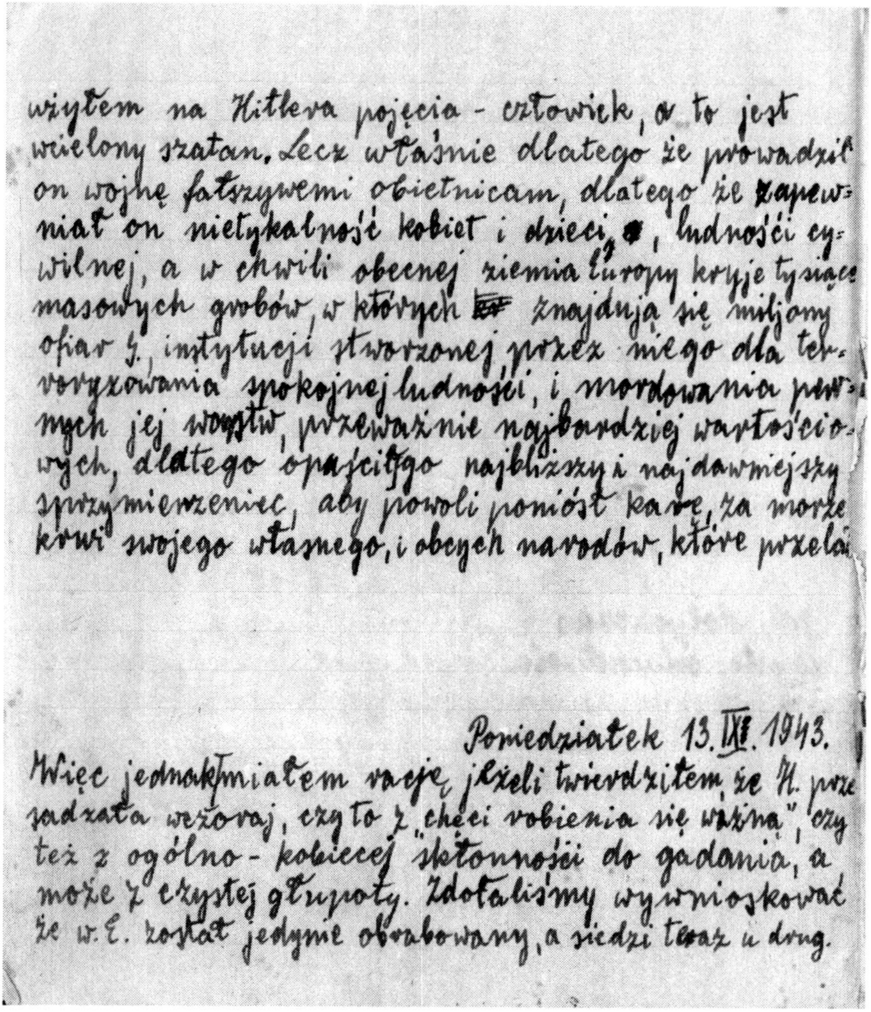

wziętem na Hitlera pojęcia - człowiek, a to jest
wcielony szatan. Lecz właśnie dlatego że prowadził
on wojnę fałszywemi obietnicam, dlatego że zapew=
niał on nietykalność kobiet i dzieci, , ludności cy-
wilnej, a w chwili obecnej ziemia Europy kryje tysiące
masowych grobów, w których znajdują się miljony
ofiar G, instytucji stworzonej przez niego dla ter-
roryzowania spokojnej ludności, i mordowania pew=
nych jej warstw, przeważnie najbardziej wartościo-
wych, dlatego opuściłgo najbliższy i najdawniejszy
sprzymierzeniec, aby powoli poniósł karę, za morze
krwi swojego własnego, i obcych narodów, które przelał

Poniedziałek 13.IX.1943.

Więc jednakmiałem rację, jeżeli twierdziłem, że H. prze
zadrżała wczoraj, czy to z chęci robienia się ważną, czy
też z ogólno-kobiecej skłonności do gadania, a
może z czystej głupoty. Zdołaliśmy wywnioskować
że w.E. został jedynie obrabowany, a siedzi teraz u drug.

Plate 4. See p. 104, Jerzyk's 'Green Notebook'.

129

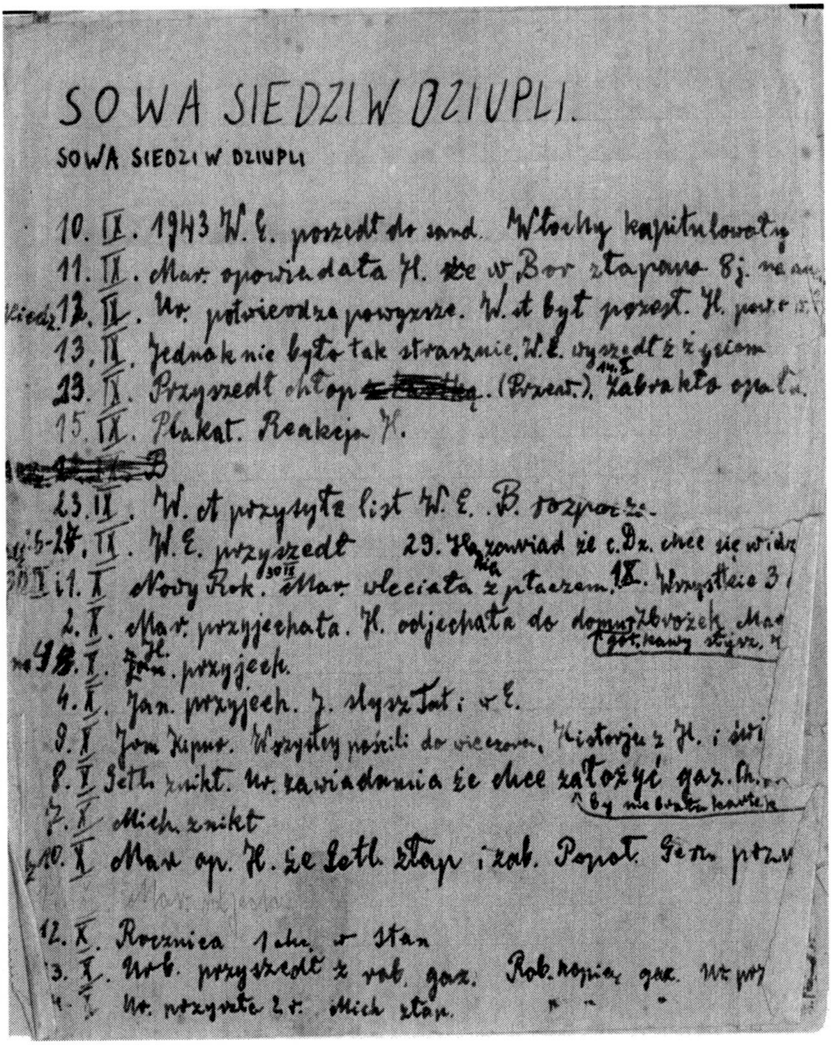

Plate 5.
See pp. 109–11, diary fragments, Jerzyk's 'Green Notebook'.

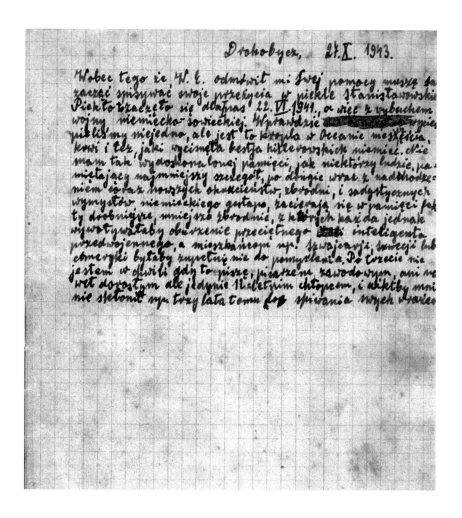

Plate 6.
See p. 101, Jerzyk's 'Pink Notebook'. Note the more careful handwriting.
These entries were more like little essays. They reflect on earlier times.

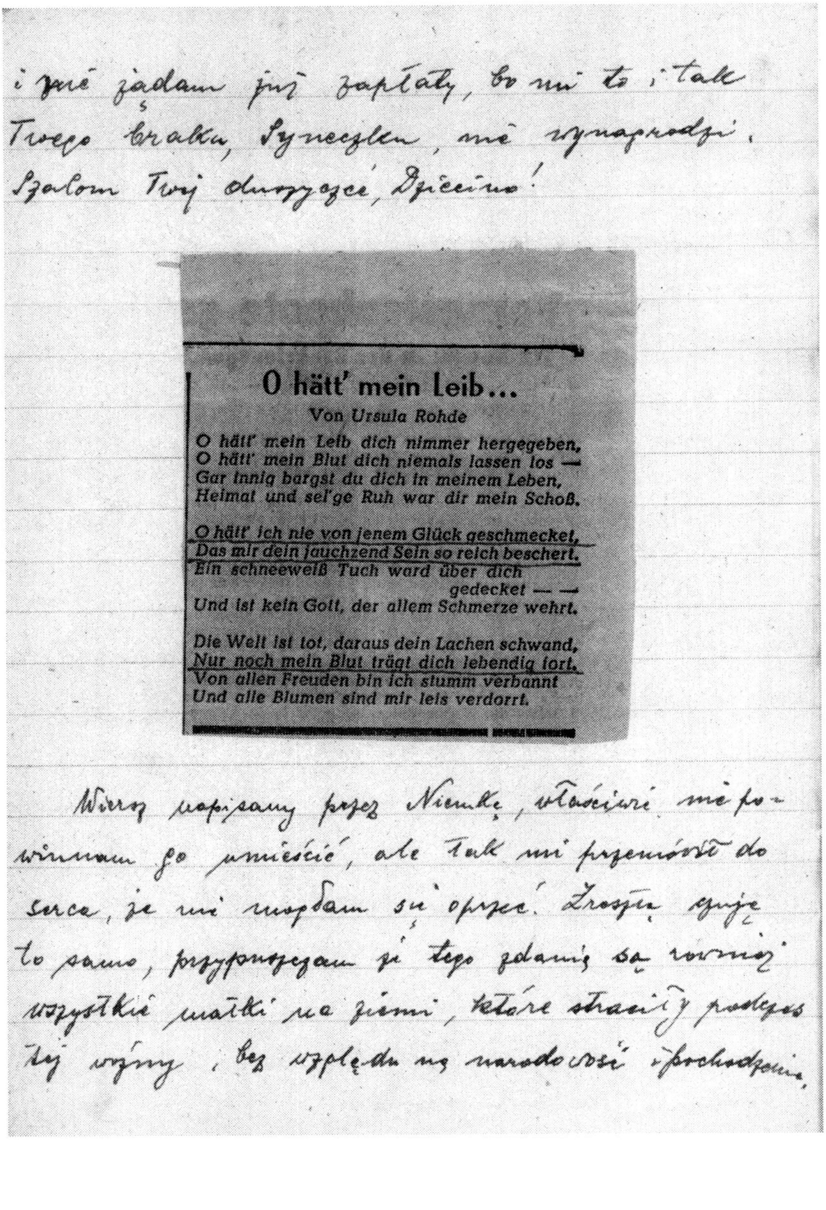

i już żądam już zapłaty, bo mi to; tak
Twego brata, Syneczku, mi wynagrodzi.
Żałom Twój dwoyozee, Dziecino!

O hätt' mein Leib...

Von Ursula Rohde

O hätt' mein Leib dich nimmer hergegeben,
O hätt' mein Blut dich niemals lassen los —
Gar innig bargst du dich in meinem Leben,
Heimat und sel'ge Ruh war dir mein Schoß.

O hätt' ich nie von jenem Glück geschmecket,
Das mir dein jauchzend Sein so reich beschert.
Ein schneeweiß Tuch ward über dich
gedecket — —
Und ist kein Gott, der allem Schmerze wehrt.

Die Welt ist tot, daraus dein Lachen schwand,
Nur noch mein Blut trägt dich lebendig fort.
Von allen Freuden bin ich stumm verbannt
Und alle Blumen sind mir leis verdorrt.

Wiersz napisany przez Niemkę, właściwie nie po-
winnam go umieścić, ale tak mi przemówił do
serca, że nie mogłam się oprzeć. Zrozie czuje
to samo, przypuszczam że tego zdania są również
wszystkie matki na ziemi, które straciły podczas
tej wojny, bez względu na narodowość i pochodzenie.

Plate 7.
See p. 50, Sophie's diary, clipping from newspaper.

132

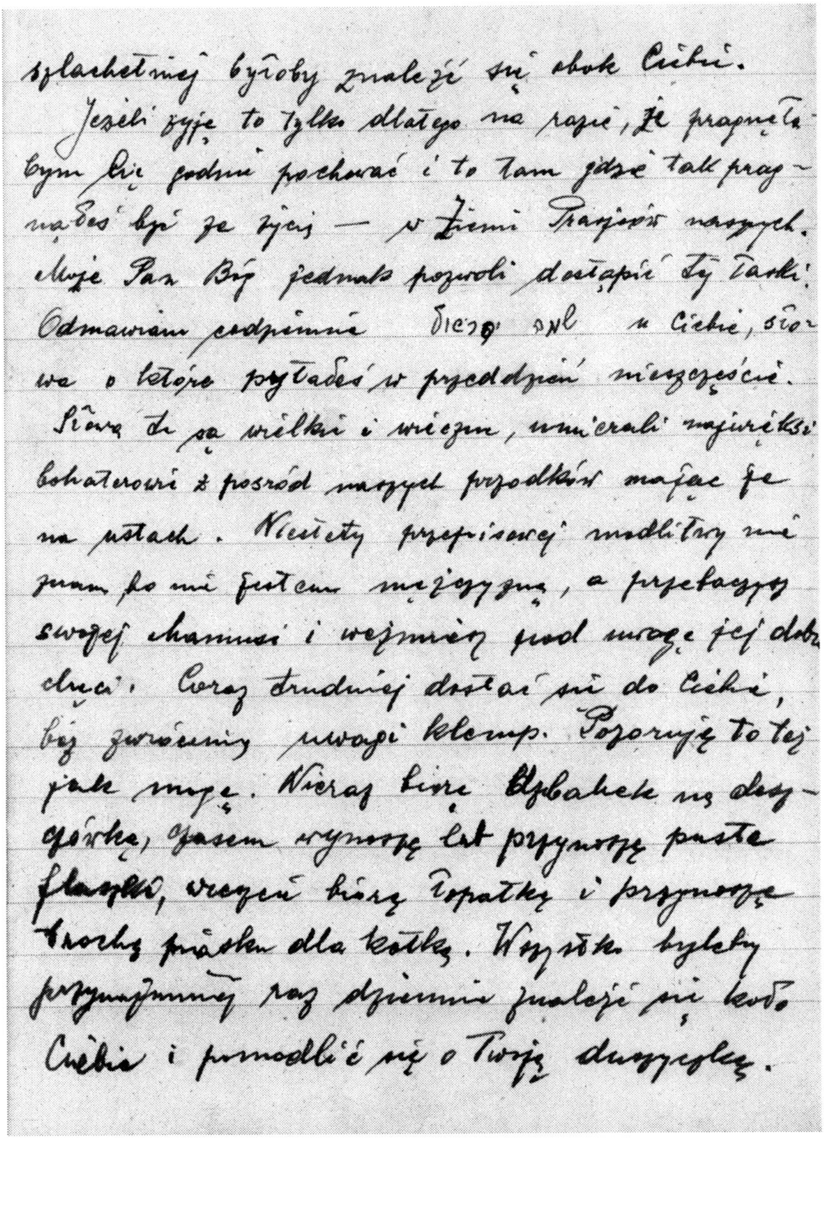

szlachetniej byłoby znaleźć się obok Ciebie.

Jeśli żyję to tylko dlatego na razie, że pragnęłabym się godnie pochować i to tam gdzie tak pragnąłeś być za życia — w Ziemi Przyjaciół naszych. Może Pan Bóg jednak pozwoli dostąpić tej łaski. Odmawiam codziennie דיבר אל za Ciebie, słowa o które pytałeś w przeddzień nieszczęścia.

Słowa te za wielki i więzień, umierali najwięksi bohaterowie z pośród naszych przodków mając je na ustach. Niestety przepisowej modlitwy nie znam, bo nie jestem mężczyzną, a przekraczając swej charakter i wejmiesz pod uwagę jej dobre chęci. Coraz trudniej dostać się do Ciebie, bez zwrócenia uwagi klemp. Pozoruję to też jak mogę. Nieraz biorę Elżbietkę na działkę, czasem wynoszę list przynoszę puste flaszki, wrogi biorę łopatkę i przynoszę trochę piasku dla kotki. Wszystko tylko przyjemniej raz dziennie znaleźć się koło Ciebie i pomodlić się o Twoją duszę szlę.

Plate 9.
See p. 45, Sophie's diary, Hebrew word spelt wrong.

134

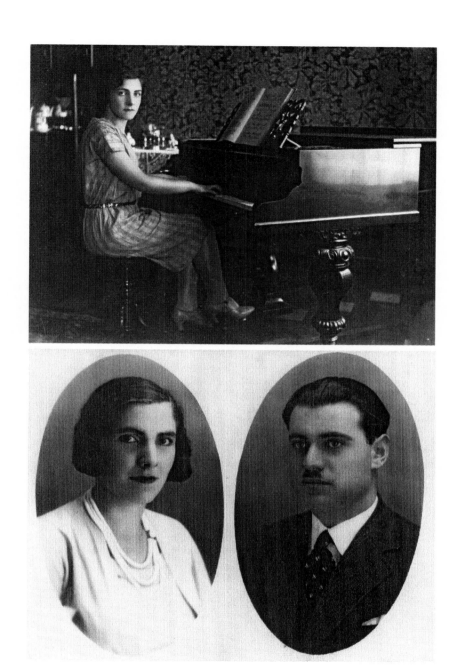

Plates 10. Sophie, around 1928–29.
Plate 11. Sophie and Izydor, early 1930; possibly their engagement photo.

Plate 12. Wedding photo, December 1930. (See p. 39.)
Plate 13. Sophie in 1930.

Plate 14. Emil and Fabian Urman, 1938, Stanisławów.
Plate 15. Emil and Hermina Urman, 1939, Stanisławów.

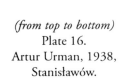

(from top to bottom)
Plate 16.
Artur Urman, 1938,
Stanisławów.

Plate 17.
Emil Urman, post-war.

Plate 18.
Izydor Urman, 1941,
Stanisławów.

Plate 19.
Jerzyk aged 1?

Plate 20.
Jerzyk aged 2?

Plate 21.
Jerzyk aged 4?
at Passover Seder.

Plate 22.
Jerzyk aged 6?

Plate 23.
Jerzyk aged 8? with initials on his
pullover, accidentally the first two
letters of the German word for *Jew*.

Plate 24.
Jerzyk aged 10, 1942, Stanisławów.

Plate 25.
Irit, Emil, and Jerzyk's second cousin, Mike Fliderbaum, 1952, Tel Aviv.

Plate 26.
Sophie and Izydor in the late 1980s. This photograph tells us that even a tragedy on the scale of Jerzyk's death can co-exist with the life force as exemplified by Sophie's writings. They chose to live. They went on to have a daughter at the end of the war. And life went on, as it does. The photo speaks to the epigraph chosen for this book from a poet who understood these matters. It is a hugely powerful photo, post-catastrophe. The sadness in their eyes interrogates us – as do, in a radically opposed way, the innocent pre-war photos, especially those of Jerzyk, which remind us of the photographs in Serge Klarsfeld's book *French Children of the Holocaust* (1996) on the deported French Jewish children: see my book *Silent Conversations* (2013) for an account.

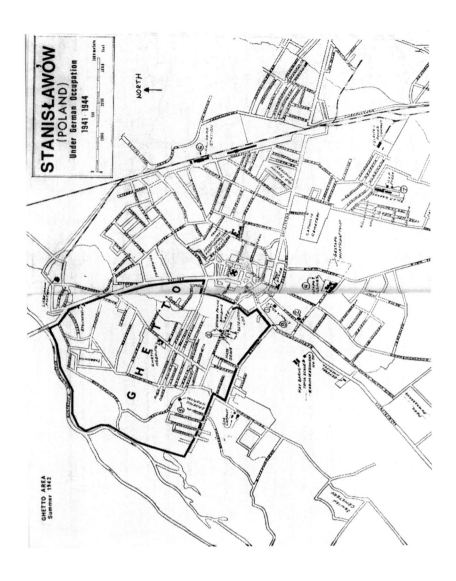

Plate 27.
Map 1 shows the ghetto area in Stanisławów (see pp. 13 and 31) in the summer of 1942. Sophie, Izydor, and Jerzyk lived on Sobieski Street just outside the
south-east corner of the ghetto near the indicated post office. My great-grand-
mother Rosa Vogel Rudolf, is buried in the cemetery indicated at the bottom
left of the map.

144

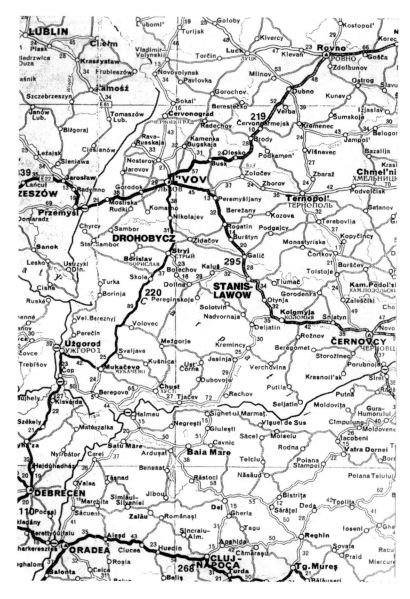

Plate 28.

Map 2 shows their home town Stanisławów and their place of hiding Drohobycz, and south-east of Stanisławów, Tłumacz, Fabian's home town. The map
also shows Brody, the birthplace of Joseph Roth, and Černovcy (Czernowitz),
birthplace of Paul Celan, Dan Pagis, Aharon Appelfeld and many other writers.

Select Bibliography to the First Edition of Jerzyk's Diary (1991), Followed by Additional Works Referred to or Consulted in the Present Work (2016)

Note concerning primary material:
Originally I only had Yad Vashem documents to work with:

03/2801 (Izydor Urman)
2274118 (Artur Urman)
03/3141 (Emil Urman)
03/2730 (Jerzy Feliks Urman)

For the present volume we were able to study the original diaries of Jerzyk and Sophie, in my possession, courtesy of Sophie and her daughter Irit, after the notebooks were found in Tel Aviv and Miami. These diaries, now very fragile, will eventually be lodged in their rightful home, Yad Vashem, Jerusalem, as agreed with Irit.

Bibliography to the First Edition (1991)

R. Ainsztein, *Jewish Resistance in Nazi-occupied Eastern Europe*, Elek, London, 1974.

J. Apensziak (ed.), *The Black Book of Polish Jewry: An Account of the Martyrdom of Polish Jewry under the Nazi Occupation*, American Federation for Polish Jews, New York, 1943.

Y. Arad (ed.), *Documents on the Holocaust*, KTAV Publishing, in association with Yad Vashem, Jerusalem, 1981.

P. Auster, *The Invention of Solitude*, Sun Books, New York, 1982.

J. Bauman, *Winter in the Morning: A Young Girl's Life in the Warsaw Ghetto and Beyond, 1930–45*, Pavanne, London, 1987.

M. Cornwall (ed.), *The Last Years of Austria–Hungary: Essays in Political and Military History, 1908–1918*, University of Exeter Press, Exeter, 1990.

L. Dawidowicz, *The War against the Jews, 1933–1945*, Holt, Rinehart and Winston, New York, 1975.

D. Dwork, *Children with a Star: Jewish Youth in Nazi Europe*, Yale University Press, New Haven, CT, 1991.

Encyclopaedia Judaica (16 volumes) [various articles], Keter, Jerusalem, 1971/72.

J. Ficowski (ed.), *Letters & Drawings of Bruno Schulz*, Harper and Row, New York, 1988.

M. Flinker, *Young Moshe's Diary*, translated by Shaul Esh, Yad Vashem, Jerusalem, 1965.

A. Frank, *The Diary of Anne Frank*, Pan Books, London, 1984.

P. Friedman, *Roads to Extinction: Essays on the Holocaust*, edited by A. J. Friedman, Jewish Publication Society of America, New York, 1980.

M. Gilbert, *The Jews of Russia: Their History in Maps and Photographs*, National Council for Soviet Jewry of the United Kingdom and Ireland, London, 1976.

M. Gilbert, *Atlas of the Holocaust*, Michael Joseph, London, 1982.

M. Gilbert, *Jewish History Atlas* (3rd edition), Weidenfeld and Nicolson, London, 1985.

M. Gilbert, *The Holocaust (The Jewish Tragedy)*, Fontana/Collins, London, 1987.

M. Greenberg, *Graves of Tzaddikim in Russia*, Shamir, Jerusalem, 1989.

D. Grossman, *See Under: Love*, translated by Betsy Rosenberg, Jonathan Cape, London, 1990.

É. Heyman, *The Diary of Éva Heyman*, translated by Moshe Kohn, Shapolsky Publishers, New York, 1988.

R. Hilberg, *The Destruction of the European Jews* (2nd edition), Holmes and Maier, New York, 1985.

D. Kahane, *Lvov Ghetto Diary*, translated by J. Michałowicz, University of Massachusetts Press, Amherst, MA, 1990.

L. Langer, *Holocaust Testimonies: The Ruins of Memories*, Yale University Press, New Haven, CT, 1991.

C. Lanzmann, *Shoah* [text of 1985 film], Paris, Pantheon, 1985.

P. R. Magocsi, *Ukraine: A Historical Atlas*, University of Toronto Press, Toronto, Ont., 1987.

M. Marrus, *The Holocaust in History*, Weidenfeld and Nicolson, London, 1988.

R. Marshall, *In the Sewers of Lvov: the Last Sanctuary from the Holocaust*, Collins, London, 1990.

C. Miłosz, *The Witness of Poetry*, Harvard University Press, Cambridge, MA, 1983.

T. Muirhead, *Out of the Ashes: A Survey of the Unhappy Lands and a Design for International Harmony*, Robert Hale, London, 1941.

C. Ozick, *The Messiah of Stockholm*, Andre Deutsch, London, 1987.

C. Ozick, *The Shawl: A Story and a Novella*, Jonathan Cape, London, 1991.

B.-C. Pinchuk, *Shtetl Jews under Soviet Rule: Eastern Poland on the Eve of the Holocaust*, Blackwell, Oxford, 1990.

P. Rawicz, *Blood from the Sky*, translated by P. Wiles, Chatto and Windus, London, 1981; revised edition by A. Rudolf, Elliott and Thompson/Menard Press, London, 2004.

E. Roith, *The Riddle of Freud*, Tavistock Publications, London, 1987.

J. Roth, *Tarabas: A Guest on Earth*, Chatto and Windus, London, 1987.

D. Rubinowicz, *The Diary of David Rubinowicz*, translated by Derek Bowman, William Blackwood, Edinburgh, 1981.

A. Rudolf, *Wine from Two Glasses*, a revised and expanded version of the 1990 Adam Lecture 'Poetry and Politics: Trust and Mistrust in Language', delivered at King's College, London, 17 October 1990, Adam Archive Publications, London, 1991.

B. Schulz, *Sanatorium under the Sign of the Hourglass*, translated by C. Wieniewska, Picador, London, 1979.

B. Schulz, *Street of Crocodiles*, translated by C. Wieniewska, Picador, London, 1980.

L. Wells, *The Death Brigade* (*The Janowska Road*), Holocaust Library, New York, 1978.

H. White, *Metahistory: The Historical Imagination in Nineteenth-Century Europe*, Johns Hopkins University Press, Baltimore, MD, 1975.

H. White, *The Content of the Form: Narrative Discourse and Historical Representation*, Johns Hopkins University Press, Baltimore, MD, 1987.

M. Winick (ed.), *Hunger Disease: Studies by the Jewish Physicians in the Warsaw Ghetto*, Wiley, New York, 1979.

J. Young, *Writing and Rewriting the Holocaust: Narrative and the Consequences of Interpretation*, Indiana University Press, Bloomington, IN, 1988.

Select Bibliography to the Present Volume (2016)

S. Bond et al. (eds), *Memorial Book of Tłumacz*, translated by Yocheved Klausner, Tłumacz Society, Tel Aviv, 1976, available at http://www.jewishgen.org/yizkor/tlumacz/tlumacz.html.

R. Char, *Feuillets d'Hypnos (1973)*, translated by Mark Hutchinson and entitled *Hypnos*, Seagull Books, London/New York/Calcutta, 2014.

J. Ficowski, *Regions of the Great Heresy: A Biographical Portrait of Bruno Schulz*, W. W. Norton, London, 2003.

J. Ficowski (ed.), *The Collected Works of Bruno Schulz*, Picador, London, 1998.

S. Klarsfeld, *French Children of the Holocaust*, New York University Press, New York, NY, 1996.

A. and M. Klonicki (Klonymus), *The Diary of Adam's Father, the Diary of Ary Klonicki (Klonymus) and His Wife Malwina, with Letters Concerning the Fate of Their Child Adam*, Ghetto Fighters House and Hakibbutz Hameuhad Publishing House, Tel Aviv, 1973.

O.-D. Kulka, *Landscapes of the Metropolis of Death: Reflections on Memory and Imagination*, Penguin, London, 2014.

P. Levi, *The Drowned and the Saved*, Abacus/Sphere, London, 1988.

J. Michlic, 'The Untold Story of Rescue Operations: Jewish Children In Nazi-Occupied Poland Helping Each Other', in Patrick Henry (ed.), *Jewish Resistance to the Nazis*, Catholic University of America Press, Washington, DC, 2014, pp. 300–18.

J. Michlic, 'The Return of the Repressed Self: Michel Glowinski's Autobiographical Wartime Writing', in *Jewish Social Studies: History, Culture, Society*, 20 (3) (2014): 131–49.

J. Michlic, 'The War Began For Me After the War: Jewish Children in Poland, 1945–1949', in Jonathan Friedman (ed.), *The Routledge History of the Holocaust* (Routledge, London / Oxford, 2011), pp. 482–97.

R. O'Neil, 'Hans Krueger in Stanisławów, Kolomyja and District', in Jason Hallgarten (ed.), *The Rabka Four: Instruments of Genocide and Grand Larceny (Poland)*, JewishGen/Yizkor Book Project, 2011, available at: http://www.jewishgen.org/yizkor/Galicia3/Galicia3.html.

G. Oppen, 'Route', in Michael Davidson (ed.), *New Collected Poems*, New Directions, New York, 2008, pp. 192–202.

M. Pinto-Duschinsky, Review of Timothy Snyder's *Black Earth: The Holocaust as History and Warning*, Bodley Head, London, 2015, in *Standpoint* 75, September 2015.

A. Rudolf, *Rescue Work: Memory and Text*, Pierre Rouve Memorial Lecture delivered at the University of Sofia, February, 2001, Leeds, *Stand* 5(3), 2004.

A. Rudolf, *Engraved in Flesh* (revised edition), Menard Press, London, 2007.

A. Rudolf, *Silent Conversations: A Reader's Life*, Seagull Books, London / New York / Calcutta, 2013

J. Semprun, *Literature or Life*, Viking, London, 1997.

D. Sierakowiak, *The Diary of Dawid Sierakowiak*, edited by Alan Adelson, translated by Kamil Turowski, Oxford University Press, New York, 1996.

B. D. Weinryb, 'Polish Jews Under Soviet Rule', in P. Meyer, B. D. Weinryb, E. Duschinsky, and N. Sylvain (eds.), *Jews in the Soviet Satellites*, Syracuse University Press, Syracuse, NY, 1953, p. 310.

Appendix

'Go into the Question: What Remains of Mark Rothstein?'

INTRODUCTION

What can we find out about a person we never knew, when we go into the question? Sometimes, it would appear, very little. Sometimes, too, as in the text that follows, some of the few details that emerged during research have turned out to be incompatible. Details are important: they are all we have. It was a given of my task to notice them. Facts, wrote Hayden White, are events under description. Technically, my particular site of remembrance on the home front was not a battlefield. The survivors could have been forgiven for thinking it was.

THE ROCKET

Mark Rothstein, my second cousin, died in a V-2 rocket raid on London, the cause of death described euphemistically as 'war operations' (not even 'enemy action') on his and his parents' death certificates. He was eleven. The V-2 was the world's first ballistic missile, brainchild of Wernher von Braun. Unmanned and unguided, these rockets were so fast you could not hear them overhead at the moment immediately before explosion, making them even deadlier and more unpredictable than the V-1. The rocket that killed Mark and his parents, Harry and Sadie, was the penultimate V-2 in the war on the homeland. It struck the flats where they lived, Hughes Mansions on Vallance Road, Stepney, at 7.21 a.m. 27 March 1945. There were a hundred and thirty-four victims, of whom a hundred and twenty were Jewish. Forty-nine people were seriously injured. The final V-2 landed on Orpington High Street a few hours later, killing one person, Ivy Millichamp, the last British civilian casualty of the Second World War. What a stroke of luck for the Nazis that the V-2, designed for random terror or, in Hitler's word, 'vengeance', hit so many of their prime enemies. In the words of the traitor Lord Haw-Haw: 'Hardest of all, the Luftwaffe will smash Stepney. I know the East End! Those dirty Jews and Cockneys will run like rabbits into their holes.'

HUGHES MANSIONS

Hughes Mansions, named after the social reformer Mary Hughes (who lived across the road next door to her Dewdrop Inn [*do drop in*] until she died in 1941) was built by Stepney Borough Council in 1928. It consisted of three identical five-storey blocks, each with thirty flats, although three of the units in the western block (giving onto Vallance Road) were and are shops. This block was damaged by the V-2 and repaired in the original style and brick shortly after the war. The tenement-style architecture is typical of London County Council social housing of the interwar period, although the flats were the latest thing in terms of fittings: for example, they all had bathrooms. The V-2 completely destroyed the middle block (where the Rothsteins lived at number 38, on one of the upper floors) and eighty per cent of the eastern block. The remaining twenty per cent was pulled down. In the 1950s, a new section was added to block one and a large second block was built.

The list of deaths reveals what one would expect: that most were in blocks two and three, although interpreting the figures is complicated by the fact that names appear in two adjacent columns: numbered flats and overall place of death, namely Hughes Mansions. Some of the victims were found outside their homes. The Rothsteins, according to a fiftieth anniversary article in the *Jewish Chronicle*, 'had run towards the stairs, dying before they could reach what no longer existed'. Sadie was discovered at 6.20 p.m., eleven hours almost to the minute after the rocket landed; her death was registered on 30 March. Mark and Harry were discovered at 7.20 p.m., twelve hours almost to the minute; their deaths were registered on 29 March.

Mark Rothstein

Mark's grandmother Sophie (née Flashtig) Rothstein was an older sister of my grandmother Fanny (née Flashtig) Rudolf. Thus Harry, Mark's father, and Henry, my father, were first cousins, and Mark and I second cousins. Sophie, judging by Harry's birth certificate (where she is Sivia), could not write, or at any rate could not write English, for her signature is a mark. Her first language will have been Yiddish, a dialect of German with Slavic elements and written in Hebrew script. Mark's younger cousin, my second cousin Denis Davis, has vague memories of Mark at occasional classic Jewish family teas on a Sunday. He had a full set of drums and he could play them.Leila Hoffman, another cousin of Mark's and second cousin of mine, remembers meeting the boy: only once, although she thinks they must have been present together on family occasions, such as weddings.

Mark was a member of Brady Boys Club, the best known of Jewish youth clubs at the time and by his day no longer based in Brady Street but in Durward Street, immediately round the corner from Hughes Mansions. He is listed on page 20 of the March 1945 issue of *The Bradian* as a new boy, 'having been elected a full member of the club after August 1944'. The new boy was dead within a few days of the Brady notice. One former member, his recently deceased contemporary Simon Palmer, remembers him as being 'a right little *lobus*' – affectionate Yiddish/Polish word for rascal.

His school friend, a neighbour from the western block (which is why he survived) and fellow-Bradian, Bernard Marks, remembers him as an extrovert and slightly spoilt only child. They would play a game called 'wally', involving throwing a ball at a high wall. Mark went to Buxton Street School until it was bombed and then transferred to Deal Street School, which became Robert Montefiore School in 1950. He may well have known the late singer Georgia Brown, a fellow pupil at Deal Street. Another school friend, Leslie Lewis (then Mendelovsky), tells me Mark was curly haired, thick set (like his father, judging by photographic evidence), and wore a lumber jacket. Leslie also says that Mark's close friends were boys from the local Roman Catholic school, some of whom would shout anti-Semitic taunts. Surprisingly, Mark even took part in fights against Jewish boys from his own school. Leslie speculates that Mark was reacting against parental expectations or pressure. This view is compatible with the suggestion that the boy was spoilt but interestingly complicated by his membership of the Jewish youth club. Another survivor, Jack Starkman, remembers Mark and another victim Ivan Saffer, but only vaguely.

MARK'S FAMILY

Mark, Sadie (née Isaacs), and Harry Rothstein and other victims of the attack are buried close by each other in the Jewish cemetery in Marlow Road, East Ham, known as the East London Cemetery. The graves have survived well. Interment was on Sunday 1 April 1945, the fourth day of Passover. Probably there was one ceremony for all the funerals and, some months later, for the tombstone settings. Their Hebrew names, as transcribed from the tombstones, are Mark: Mordechai son of Hirsch; Sadie: Sarah daughter of Mordechai; Harry: Hirsch son of Shlomo (i.e. Solomon). Mark's tomb is in section R, row 21 number 1346. Thus, as the Anglicisation of the children of immigrants proceeded, an initial trace of origin remained. The victims of the V-2 attack came unstuck in place and time; the wrong place at the wrong time: Lord Haw-Haw's Stepney.

Harry's tombstone says he was forty-one, but, according to the 1911 census, he was born in 1900; his death certificate, too, says he was forty-five and his birth certificate gives his date of birth as 17 March 1900. Sadie's tombstone says she was forty-six. Their marriage certificate of 24 June 1927 says they were twenty-eight when they were married, but Harry was twenty-seven. Mark was only eleven – according to his birth certificate he was born on 30 May 1933 – but the tombstone says he was twelve. On his marriage certificate, Harry is listed as a commercial traveller. Later, we learn from his death certificate, he was a cinema owner. In between, according to Mark's birth certificate, he was a draper's collector. On Sadie's death certificate, he is not an owner but a 'cinema manager' and, indeed, according to press reports, he was the manager of the New Pavilion Picture Palace in Poplar. A search on the Internet reveals that the cinema was damaged in a V-2 rocket attack on 24 March and temporarily closed – only three days before the attack that killed Harry.

In 1933, Mark's birth certificate tells us, the family was living at 292 Commercial Road. According to the electoral register, they were still living there in October 1939. The Great Synagogue, a few doors away at 262 Commercial Road (where Harry and Sophie were married), was a constituent member of the Federation of Synagogues, and yet the Rothsteins are buried in Marlow Road, a United Synagogue cemetery. This could mean that the couple joined a local constituent of the more anglicised United Synagogue after they married, perhaps when their son was born, but, more likely, according to Denis Davis, niceties of affiliation were permitted to be disregarded in the extreme situation of war.

THE PRESS

The day of the V-2 attack, 27 March 1945, was the thirtieth birthday of my mother Esther [*née Rosenberg*] Rudolf. I was aged about two and a half and she was three months pregnant with my sister Ruth. In researching the fate of my relatives on that day, seventy years ago, I assumed initially that the attack would have been reported the next day, perhaps even headlined, in the press, and that my parents would have read about it in *The Times*, which was their newspaper of choice along with the *News Chronicle*, judging by their reading matter recalled from my childhood a few years later. But I was forgetting about press censorship, imposed for reasons of morale and security. There was no mention of the attack until 11 May, three days after VE Day, when with unconscious irony from the point of view of the East End, Hughes Mansions first appears in an article in *The Times* headlined 'Victory Holiday Scenes'. The surviving block and the bombsite to its rear were visited by the King and Queen and their two daughters on that day.

The *News Chronicle* had reported on 4 April that all the signs were that the V-bombing was over, otherwise nothing. Nor, unless I missed something on the microfilm at the British Library newspaper reading room in Colindale, did the *Jewish Chronicle* publish a report until 4 May, several weeks after the bomb attack. We learn that this was the 'second largest death-roll in the seven months of Southern England's ordeal by V-2s'. On the same day, which was probably not a coincidence, three articles were published in the *East London Advertiser*, the local newspaper. We learn that the first doodlebugs (in the popular phrase) or flying bombs (as the V-1 was named by government fiat in April 1943) landed on Grove Road, Stepney, on 13 June 1944. Now, on 27 March 1945, Stepney endured the final day of the V-2 bombings.

HUGHES MANSIONS AND MY GRANDMOTHER

The wedding of my father's youngest brother Leon was celebrated on 25 March, two days before the bombing raid. Denis, who was nine years old, remembers drinking lemonade under a table at the reception with his younger brother Stanley, aged six. It is certain that Harry, Sadie, and Mark were present. Leon's late widow Freda, according to my cousin Angela, recalled that while on honeymoon in Torquay, Leon (after hearing an allusion to air raids on the BBC?) phoned my father and learnt about the tragedy. However, Denis reckons that his mother Becky Davis (née Rothstein) would have phoned my father. My father would then have phoned Leon and Becky would have phoned her and Harry's brother, Joe Rothstein, Mark's uncle. Joe's daughter Leila tells me he rushed to London from Worthing after being informed about the air raid. As we know, the bodies were not discovered and identified by Joe until many hours later.

My mother once told me that my grandmother, her mother-in-law Fanny, Mark's great aunt, wanted my father and her not to leave the East End for pastures north-west following their marriage (in 1938), but to stay near the two sets of parents, who lived in Stepney and Bishopsgate, respectively. Bobba 'Dolf (as I called my grandmother) thought Henry and Esther should start married life in Hughes Mansions, which in her opinion was the best and smartest place in the East End. Had she visited Hughes Mansions? If so, it could not have been the Rothsteins' flat, since my parents married the year before the Rothsteins moved there. Perhaps it was hearsay. Whatever, the young couple, determined for their own reasons to leave the East End, moved to Flat Three, 38 Greencroft Gardens in Swiss Cottage for about three years. From Swiss Cottage, and probably renting from Henry's uncle and first cousin once removed, Ike Flashtig, they moved to 46 Boyne Avenue in Hendon, where I was conceived. Henry and Esther ended up in 41 Middleway, Hampstead Garden Suburb, NW11, a few months before my birth on 6 September 1942 at the Salvation Army Mothers Hospital in Hackney. My mother lived in Middleway for sixty years. Fortunately for me and for her and for my father, they had chosen not to live in Hughes Mansions.

CONCLUSION

How little is known of Mark. He is remembered, and that is already something. A thousand miles from London, Jerzy Feliks Urman, also a second cousin, died (by his own hand) in November 1943, also as a result of enemy action. He was almost exactly the same age as Mark. I have far more information about his life in hiding in western Ukraine than I do about Mark's life in London… My two cousins belong in the same book, which is their memorial. The world shows no sign of learning from cruel tragedies such as these. But hope, which is not to be confused with optimism, is a prophylactic against despair, and so I hope against hope, or rather, hope against despair, that the world can be repaired, speedily and in our days.

BIBLIOGRAPHY

A. Calder, *The People's War: Britain, 1939–45*, Jonathan Cape, London, 1969.

C. Campbell, *Target London: Under Attack from the V-Weapons during WWII*, Little Brown, London, 2012.

G. Brown [the singer Georgia Brown], 'One Pair of Eyes: Who Are the Cockneys Now' (a documentary). BBC, London, 1968, available at: www.youtube.com/watch?v=-7uW7koB7pw#t=2428.

M. Lazarus, *A Club Called Brady*, New Cavendish Books, London, 1996.

L. Lewis, 'The Last Rocket', *Jewish Chronicle*, 3 February 1995.

Home Office, 'Air Raids: Incident Reports Stepney', *Documents HO 186/2420* [public record], National Archives, Kew, London, 1941–45.

H. Pollins, 'Jewish Civilian Deaths during World War II in the Metropolitan Borough of Stepney' [complete Hughes Mansions death list], available at: http://www.jewishgen.org/jcr-uk/static/stepney_civilians_killed_in_wwii.pdf.

W. G. Romney, *The East End Then and Now*, After the Battle, London, 1997.

W. G. Sebald, *On the Natural History of Destruction*, Hamish Hamilton, London, 2003.

Y. Sheridan, *From Here to Obscurity*, Tenterbooks, London, 2001.

H. White, *Metahistory: The Historical Imagination in Nineteenth-Century Europe*, Johns Hopkins University Press, Baltimore, MD, 1975.

ACKNOWLEDGEMENTS

Thanks for their help to my second cousins, Denis Davis and Leila Hoffman, and my cousin Angela Reuben. Thanks to my friend Michael Lazarus for pointing me in the direction of Betty Wess, who pointed me in the direction of Lou Lawrence (and the page of former Bradians on Facebook), as well as Simon Palmer, who remembered Mark. Thanks to David Walker of *The Cable*, the magazine of the Jewish East End Celebration Society (JEECS, whose president until his death in 2014 was my old friend Professor Bill Fishman), who suggested Lord Haw-Haw as a source and put me in touch with Yoel Sheridan, who in turn supplied the list of 'new boys' signed by him as he then was, Julius Shrensky. More thanks to David Walker with much help in reformatting my article after it appeared in *The Cable*. A letter from me seeking information about Hughes Mansions and published in the *Jewish Chronicle* eventually led to contact with Bernard Marks: my thanks to him. Thanks also to my nephew Nick Bell, whose suggestion of a letter to the taxi-drivers' magazine led me to Joe Emden, who led me to Leslie Lewis. And to Shelly Small who put me onto Jack Starkman.

Thanks too to the United Synagogue (Archives and Burial Society) and Findagrave photographer Geoffrey Gillon; to Clive Bettington of JEECS; to Malcom Barr-Hamilton and colleagues at Tower Hamlets Local History Library and Archives in Bancroft Road, where during several visits I checked photographs, ordinance survey maps, press cuttings, and electoral registers; to Mike Brooke of the *East London Advertiser*; to an anonymous professional genealogist in the British Library; and, in particular, to Stephanie Lafferty formerly of Enfield Public Libraries (and her son Chris). Getty Images supplied the photograph of the bomb-damaged Hughes Mansions on p. 158, which is their copyright.

Thanks to Deryn Rees-Jones and Elaine Feinstein for their comments on an early draft, and to Clive Sinclair and Paul Pines for their comments on a later one. Thanks, too, to Adrian Blamires and Peter Robinson, editors of *The Arts of Peace*, to David Walker, editor of *The Cable* and to Gerald Jacobs my old *patron* and books editor of the *Jewish Chronicle*, where this essay first appeared in slightly different versions from the one printed here (and somewhat shortened in the *Jewish Chronicle*). Unless new material turns up, the text is now as definitive as I can make it. Finally, for permission to use photos, thanks are offered to Tower Hamlets Local History Library and Archives, to Geoffrey Gillon and the Essex Commemoration Project, and to Leila Hoffman.

Plate 1: Hughes Mansions, 1929, the year after it was built.
Plate 2: Hughes Mansions, 27 March, 1945.

Plate 3:

Mark Rothstein is just visible in this picture from the Brady Boys Club. He died within ten days of being listed (see Plate 4, right) as a new member of the club.

From Radio Mechanic to Radio Officer
or Six Months Hard Labour

I first decided to become a Radio Officer in the M.N. in March, 1943. The procedure seemed very simple and straightforward. First of all I went to the school and obtained the necessary forms, filled them in, getting three people to vouch for me, and paid the entrance fee.

Three days later, a letter was sent to me from the General Post Office telling me that I could not become a Radio Officer as my parents were not British. I immediately phoned up the G.P.O. and indignantly informed them that my parents were both naturalised British subjects and so a week later they sent me permission to attend the school.

The boys in the school were all very friendly (I call them boys although their ages ranged between 17 and 43), and the two masters enjoyed nothing better than arguing with them about all the news of the day. (Those two masters were always against everything that the government said, but they were Englishmen through and through).

And so the days wore on, for 6 long weary months with one thought always uppermost in my mind—that, when I acquired the knowledge, I would fulfil an ambition of mine—namely to go to sea.

I began a three day exam. with a bad attack of nerves and finished up by passing with three other "boys" (out of 17 entrants).

I took a week visual signalling course and a special gunnery course and then, armed with the three certificates, I went to sign on with a shipping company and get a ship (fully expecting to be away within two weeks).

Four months have now elapsed and I am still waiting for my ship to come in. It was just my luck to pass when there was a large drop in the demand for Radio Officers. But, I have my certificates and my uniforms so I'll just wait patiently, ignoring the cracks of the boys about me being a Chief Cabin Boy, until I am called.

SIDNEY KATZ

Idiot or Brady Boy?

If you can buy a new cravat all green with spots of red.

If you can do a tango although you're almost dead.

If you can sell your purple shirt at half the price you bought it.

If you find a page of coupons, and give it up as if you hadn't bought it.

If you can smoke a cigarette right to the very tip.

If you try to keep it in your mouth until you burn your lip.

If you can do all this and more and still retain your joy.

You're just a raving lunatic, or else a Brady Boy.

R. USSISKIN

New Boys

The Club is pleased to welcome the following boys who have been elected full members since August:

Sidney Cohen   Monty Losowsky
Stanley Jonescu   David Glatt
Harry Marks   Henry Harris
Martin Donnelly   Gerald Soper
Philip Hatter   Jeffrey Cohen
David Podolsky   Irvin Stickler
Mark Rothstein   Cyril Pyzer
Jack Forman   Joseph Bolle
Alfred Kantrowitz   Ephraim Franks
Cyril Stickler   Jack Daren
Tony Botsman   Raymond Burman
Ronald Chornin   Cedric Paul Joseph
Sidney Jacobs   Harry Sass
Isaac Shaposnian   Alan Cohen
Mick Goldberg   Alan Landsberg

Published at the Brady Boys' Club, Durward Street, E.1 and Printed by D. Fisterian, 193 Brick Lane, E.2

In Memoriam

A Memorial Service for the twenty-one members of the Brady Clubs and Settlement who were killed in a recent V bomb incident in Vallance Road, E.1, took place at the Girls' Club on Tuesday, April 17th, 1945.

The Members of the Associated Clubs who lost their lives were:—

Every day we hear of people being killed on the battle-fronts, of defence-less citizens being massacred in con-centration camps, of communities be-ing wiped out en masse and our finer instincts revolt. We see photographs of tortured peoples and we feel literally sick. We have these reactions because the atrocities we hear of and see, clash with every-thing we have been taught to be right and proper But the loss of this hu-man life may not leave an empty place in our hearts.

The death of the twenty-one mem-bers of the Brady Clubs and Settle-ment is a personal tragedy to us all. One could sense the feeling of personal loss at the Memorial Service. The solemn and deliberate way in which everyone sang the psalms was a sure proof how they had been affected.

Such tragedies tend to make one lose faith in God. "The faith," to quote Mr Basil Henriques, "which

---

BRADY BOYS' CLUB

Pilot-Officer GERALD MANTUS
HAROLD RABIN
LOUIS RABIN
MARK ROTHSTEIN
IVAN SAFFER
Corporal KEVE WINGRAD
MAURICE WINGRAD

BRADY GIRLS' CLUB

LILY BEAVER
BLANCHE COHEN
CISSIE COHEN
IRENE COHEN
LILY FREEMAN
LILY HARRIS
ANITA NATHAN

BRADY JUNIOR CLUB AND PLAY CENTRE

SHIRLEY BEAVER
HELEN BRADLOFSKY
ROSALIE GREEN
JACK GROVES
BENITA NOBLE
HAROLD NOBLE
MAVIS SOLOMONS

---

has kept Jewry alive during all the trials and tribula-tions of the past and from which one can receive a consola-tion—that nothing human or tangible can give."

Although it is im-possible to make up for the loss of dear ones, Miss Miriam Moses has been able to make the grief of the mourners a little easier to bear For this grand work Mr Sam Ansell thanked her on be-half of all present at the service.

Our heartfelt sympathy goes out to all the bereaved. We feel sure that those of us who remain will learn from the short lives of the victims to appreciate more those who are near to us.

To those who have passed on we send this message "We will carry on, we will see that the evil forces which have caused your death and so much misery will never rise again, we will fight for goodness and peace, we will fight until love is supreme."

J SHRENSKY

Plate 5:
The *Brady Bulletin* memorial page listing members killed by the V-2 raid.

Plate 6:
Solomon Rothstein and
his daughter Rebecca
Rothstein (later Becky
Davis), grandfather and
aunt of Mark.

Plate 7:
Joe (left) and Harry Rothstein, uncle and father of Mark.

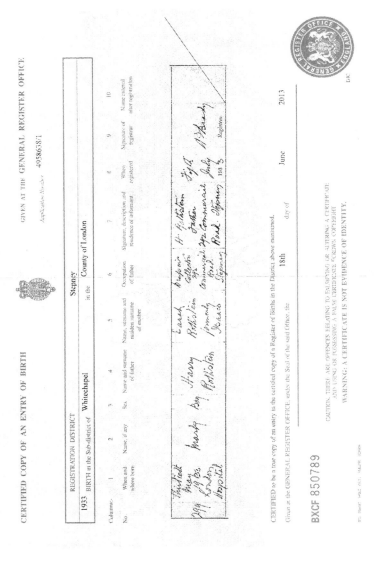

Plate 8:
Birth certificate of Mark Rothstein.

162

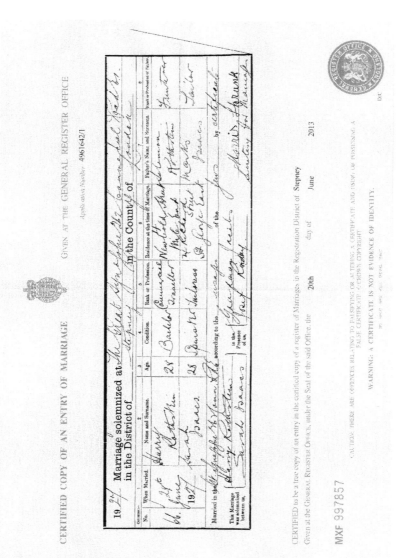

Plate 9:
Marriage certificate of Harry and Sarah (Sadie) Rothstein.

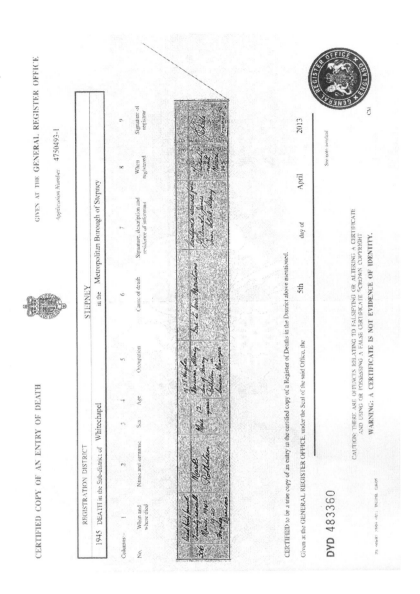

Plate 10:
Death certificate of Mark Rothstein.

164

Plate 11:
The graves of Mark Rothstein and his parents at
Marlow Road cemetery, East London.

Lightning Source UK Ltd.
Milton Keynes UK
UKOW02f2012020516

273424UK00001B/12/P